Dream Big

Think It!
Work It!
DO IT!

WINNING IN LIFE AND BUSINESS

JOYCE RICE

Think it! Work it! Do it! Winning in Life and Business

Copyright © 2019 by Joyce Rice.

All rights reserved.

No part of this publication or the information in it may be quoted from or reproduced in any form by means such as printing, scanning, photocopying or otherwise without prior written permission of the copyright holder.

Dedication

This book is dedicated to my greatest blessing: my daughter Rhonda. Thank you for being the balancing force in my life, as well as being a creative, talented, and loyal partner in our decades-long business. You will never realize the full extent of my love and gratitude.

And to my parents, who are still alive and with me in my heart, for being excellent role models who taught me responsibility, integrity, and persistence which have served me well throughout life. God blessed me richly!

Contents

Foreword 1

Section One - THINK IT! 3

BEGINNING TO END
Ignore obstacles and embrace growth. 5

THINK BIG, AIM HIGH
Creating what you desire. 9

QUIET TIME
A time to honor or reset your compass. 13

THOUGHTS AND FEELINGS
How to keep thoughts and feelings positive. 15

EVENTS, DESIRES, DREAMS
One step at a time to amazing success. 19

BELIEFS AND DESIRES
The power of beliefs and desires. 23

SELF-WORTH & STRENGTHS
Assess, reset or build, and utilize. 27

ATTITUDE
You control your attitude as it controls your life. 31

PREPARATION/COURAGE/CONFIDENCE
Preparation leads. 35

Section Two - WORK IT! 39

CHARTING YOUR COURSE
Assess Who, What, Where with clarity, enthusiasm, and patience. 41

TIME
Investing or spending?.. 45

BASICS
All is built on them.. 49

RISKS
Embrace risks.. 51

CONCENTRATE AND RELAX
Key to learning and performing... 55

VISUALIZATION
More than a mind's eye vision of dreams, actions, and outcomes.
.... 57

VALUE OF LOSING
A win in learning. 61

MENTORS
Precious and life-changing... 65

INNOVATION
The secret to success. 69

RESPONSIBLE AND RESPECTFUL
Are intertwined for success and happiness................................. 77

INTEGRITY
Like attitude, encompasses and affects every part of your life. . 81

SUPPORTING ACT
A valued perspective for keeping ego in check. 85

FULFILLING A NEED
From a vision to building, adapting, leading and supporting to
fulfill a need. 87

EVERYDAY LEADING
Simply stepping out in front with an objective and sharing what
you know. 91

21st CENTURY LEADERSHIP

Be attentive to change and valued principles 95

Section Three - DO IT! 101

OVERCOMING FEAR
It is possible! 103

PROBLEM TO ADVANTAGE
Accept the gift and build on it. 109

HABITS
Enemies or allies? 111

TOTAL FITNESS
Mandatory for excellent health and for elevating success 115

COMPETITION
No one is exempt. Competition stokes the fire within. 123

REINVENTING AND FULFILLING EVER-EXPANDING NEEDS
Capitalize on your knowledge, aptitudes, and strengths. 127

CREATE
Be grateful for creativity and protective. 131

COMMUNICATION
Clear, open and kind. 135

EXCELLENCE
Strive for excellence and value. 143

CHOICES & FATE
Lead to your destiny. 147

I DARE YOU
.... 151

YOUR FUTURE
It's your decision. 153

Acknowledgment 159
About the Author 161

Foreword

This book is about how YOU can reach and exceed your desires, goals, and dreams... How to Win in Life and Win in Business!

My purpose, for many decades, is to help people find and maximize their talents to reach their ever-expanding potential. **The strength of associations and businesses lies in elevating and utilizing every member's potential. We all have untapped potential. Let's begin the tapping.**

As a child, I believed I could go as far and high as I desired. I never thought *who* you were or *where* you came from was an advantage or disadvantage. At age seventeen and with years of preparation, I competed nationally with over 20,000 other girls and won! **Success, your success, is determined by your desire, mindset, and preparation.**

I've continued to use the principles proven to elevate performance levels throughout my life, adapting and applying them to fit the endeavor and desired outcome. From professional speaking and entertaining world-wide to building a business that created a national movement, the principles work! Professionally and personally!

Perhaps you want to create positivity in your life, overcome fear, gain confidence, be more creative and innovative, embrace challenges, increase happiness—all that and much more is in this book. The *how-tos* are under the respective three sections of my action plan, Think it! Work it! Do it!—the universal action plan and mantra used by private individuals to business tycoons for elevating performance levels and overall success.

You are capable of fulfilling your desires, goals, and dreams. Use this book as your guide and be in control of your life, a life filled with success and happiness!

Ready, Set, Go!!

Section One

THINK IT!

BEGINNING TO END
Ignore obstacles and embrace growth.

When I entered this world, it was a very different era than today. Like many babies in rural Iowa, the doctor delivered me at home. I came on Father's Day and a month early. A cousin nursed my mother back to health and wouldn't give up on me surviving. Several months later all was well. I like to think a difficult beginning builds strength and courage for the long run.

My parents had faith that their hard work and Mother Nature's kindness would provide enough to pay the mortgage on their small farm. An oil heater heated our four-room home. There was no running water. We pumped water from a well in the front yard and carried it in pails to the house. The wood cookstove had a water reservoir. When my mother wasn't outside doing chores, she was cooking so the reservoir water kept warm. I remember neighbors and family liking my mother's cooking. Everyone loved her sour cream devil's food cake with fudge frosting.

I had two sets of grandparents and a set of great-grandparents. My great-grandpa had a large collection of Native American relics, weapons, and stones used to make tools, clothing, and prepare food. He would set me on his knee and show me how to use the various stones. He told me stories about growing up along the Des Moines River with his Indian friends. Stories about how fast they could run, how they stood so straight and tall, how beautiful the maidens were. I loved the images his stories painted. I added to my prayers, "Please make me an Indian princess."

My grandpa who lived in town came one Saturday afternoon to take my brother and me to see a movie! Loving all the Indian stories, I was ready for more excitement. The theatre was dark and mysterious. The seats were very soft and big. I remember my feet extending to the edge of the seat. When I sat back, the seat folded up. Grandpa told me to sit on the edge of the seat and it wouldn't fold up. Grandpas are smart.

The Roy Rogers movie opened my world to cowboys, horses, and good guys and bad guys. I loved Roy Rogers! I could tell he was just like my father. He was always honest and kept good people safe. My father didn't have Trigger, but that was okay, he knew everything, just like Roy.

I was painfully shy and seldom said anything. When I talked, few could understand me. When excited, no one could. The excitement of seeing my first movie made it impossible to understand a word I said. My father would always listen and smile in agreement. When he did chores, I would hold on to his finger, if one was free, and tried my best to keep up. He took long quick steps. He always made me feel I was helping.

When he went to town for something, I'd be eager for his return home. Then, I would squeeze between my parents as they talked so I could hear everything. One day he said to my mother, "I talked to the doctor. He told me how he could fix Joyce's talking. He would cut that little part under her tongue so she could speak and everyone could understand her."

I couldn't believe what I had just heard! I looked for my mother's response. She didn't say a word, but her face showed the horror I felt. Two days later I was speaking as plain as any 5-year-old. Who would have known I was capable of speaking plainly? Only my father knew. He knew and had the courage to call my bluff.

My father never talked to the doctor but believed I would need an option scarier than speaking. He didn't want me debilitated by shyness and gave me an option. The shyness didn't leave, but I learned how to gain control and eliminate debilitating consequences.

As a young girl, my favorite chore was bringing in the milk cows for the evening milking. I would walk through the lot, across the creek, up the big hill, and find them grazing on the other side. The quiet solitude gave me a welcoming environment to imagine and dream, accompanied by nature and its many living creatures. I learned the rewards of responsibility and achievement, but it was the hill that kept speaking to me, "Joyce, there is more and you are free to go as far and high as you desire." With the solid earth beneath my feet, I was free, free to imagine the wind carrying me to a magical unknown.

Leaning into the wind with outstretched arms, I welcomed the mild balmy air. I hesitated at the very top of the hill overlooking the surrounding landscape of fenced fields and pastures below me. The hill was the top of my world and filled me with feelings of freedom and wonderment. What is beyond? What is it like? When will I know?

For decades I have fearlessly traveled the world creating, innovating and risking my way to success. Come with me as I share valuable life lessons, the lessons that formed my Action Plan and Proven Principles to winning in life and in business.

Be empowered with confidence and learn how to:

- Maximize your talents.

- Rise to the top and beyond your goals and dreams.

- Reach and utilize your ever-expanding potential.

- Live life with purpose, happiness, passion, and joy!

Why elevate and utilize your potential? Because we all know,

> *"The value of each segment shapes the value of the whole."*

The truth is, who you are or where you start does not limit your success. Your success is about your hunger. Your hunger fuels your commitment, focus, and perseverance. How strong is your hunger, your desire?

THINK BIG, AIM HIGH
Creating what you desire.

Thinking only of the possible does not foster the impossible. Think Big and Aim High—beyond the possible! Allow yourself to be outrageous, such as my saying, "I plan on living to be 120." When people look at me, half in disgust, I just smile and say, "So far it's working great!"

I'm a believer that we don't wear out, we rust out without use! We must keep moving physically and mentally. Without activity, purpose, and hope our spirit dies. Once the spirit dies, the body will follow.

I've been young, middle-aged, and guess I'm still middle-aged since I'm living to be 120. Seriously, age is only a number. Don't accept others' pegging you as too young or too old. It's your decision. At all ages, we must do what we like and what gives our life meaning.

Esquire's 2016 interview with Clint Eastwood, still vital, vibrant and pushing himself creatively, proves the point. He is a reminder that we must keep evolving. Eastwood said, "I don't look at my life too much. I'm always looking forward."

When asked, "How do you stay vital? You're 86 and still doing great work."

He replied, "You are as young or old as you feel, as young or old as you want to be. There's an old saying I heard from a friend. People ask him, 'Why do you look so good at your age?' He'll say, 'Because I never let the old man in.'" Eastwood continued with, "The truth is, it is in your mind, how far you let him in. In fact, don't even let him be out there."

In 425 BC, Aristotle wrote that if you want to be virtuous, you only have to act as if you're virtuous. Now known as the 'as if' technique. William James picked up the same concept in the 1800s. He was a psychology professor with an intense interest in the mind-body connection. He knew that when people were happy, they smiled and that when people were unhappy, they frowned. James believed the opposite could be true. His findings were published in his book *Techniques of Psychology*. He was often quoted as saying,

> *"If you want a quality,*
> *act as if you already have it."*

In the 1970s, James' work was discovered by James Laird, a psychology student. He forced his face into a smile, held it and felt happier. He wanted to test it on others so invited volunteers to participate in his research. Laird told them he was connecting electrodes to various parts of their faces to measure electrical changes that occurred when they either smiled or frowned. They were instructed to manipulate the electrodes by pulling them down at the corners of their mouth into a frown or pulling them toward the back of their face into a smile. The electrodes were fake, but the results were amazing. Those who forced their face into a smile said they felt considerably happier and those who frowned reported feeling sad and angry.

We used to think the brain was in charge of everything, that our feelings originated from within. Now we know better. Research has proven time and time again that we can stimulate the feelings we want by acting 'as if' we already have them. Famous names like Anthony Robbins and Richard Wiseman latched onto it, giving it a modern spin. Wiseman even wrote a book about it: *The As if Principle*.

Your body and brain work together fulfilling your goals. Synergy compounds and escalates the results. When you have physical, mental and emotional health, how quickly you move forward will amaze you.

You create your life. What you expect to happen is what your creative capacity goes to work to produce. You create what you expect.

"High expectations are the key to everything."
-Sam Walton, Walmart founder

QUIET TIME
A time to honor or reset your compass.

I am grateful to have had an abundance of quiet time with its many rewards.

In the quietness, you can hear your heart, it's beating, and its desires. In the quietness, your instincts will talk to you and guide you. Listen, hear! In the quietness, you can reason with your overzealous, ancient fight-or-flight-thinking brain. The brain's sole intent is to protect you from danger and warn you against all that may make you uncomfortable. Change is uncomfortable. However, if you do what you have always done, you will get what you have always gotten. Comfort is the enemy of progress. Acknowledge your brain with all its warnings and say, "I hear your warnings, but I prefer to listen to and be guided by my heart and my instincts."

Quiet time allows for reflection on your recent personal history. If you don't know where you were and don't assess what you learned, how can you adjust, adapt and change OR build on what was successful to use now and in the future?

How can you express gratitude without taking time for reflection?

Treasure your quiet time. It is free of distractions and the influences of people on a different path. A time to reflect and hear your heart. A time to develop clarity and see clearly your purpose as a unique individual.

We all are miracles, gold mines of unimaginable capabilities waiting to be released. Be quiet and listen to your heart. Be still and feel your instincts. Know you are a one-of-a-kind individual with unique talents, desires, and purposes. You are the caretaker and decision-maker. How far and high will you go?

THOUGHTS AND FEELINGS
How to keep thoughts and feelings positive.

The most valuable lesson I ever learned was in the potato patch. A very unlikely place, I agree, but you never know where you may learn something that will benefit you greatly throughout your life. This lesson learned and activated will make life easier, more enjoyable and the impossible possible.

It was on the farm in the fall and nearly dusk. The air was damp and chilly. We had finished chores and were to pick up the potatoes my father had plowed out earlier. The rows were long to this 7-year-old. The moldy odor of the damp soil and potatoes made me feel nauseous.

My mother was already well down her row when she noticed my pokiness and gloomy demeanor. She hollered, "Joyce, hurry up, it's going to get dark."

I said, "But, Mom, I hate picking up potatoes more than anything in the world. The worms!"

I had thought the worms might divert her, instead, there she was standing in front of me saying, "You can learn to like doing anything—it's all up to you. Make it fun, make it a game! See how many you can pick up, how fast, how many big ones. And think how nice it will be when it's done."

She rushed back to finish her row, then started up mine to meet me. I tried to see how fast I could pick up potatoes so she didn't have many of mine to do—and to get done before dark. It was exciting! My mother had given me freedom from being miserable doing a distasteful job that must be done. More importantly, I had learned that I could control my thoughts and feelings. And you can too!

The James-Lange theory of psychology says—by acting and behaving in a cheerful manner, your feelings will rush to keep up. So why wait for the mood?

I have found the farmer was right. He used only one spur on his horse, assuming if one side gets going, the other side will follow. In much the same way, if you make your actions and activities positive and cheerful—your moods and attitudes will follow. Just as both sides of a horse move together, so do your actions and activities, moods and attitudes. Positive produces positive!

A positive attitude is vital to your success, personally and professionally! Your attitude determines the level of your potential. Your attitude produces the intensity of your activity and predicts the quality of the result you receive. The good news is, you are in control of your attitude. And with attitudes being contagious, you can make yours worth catching!

When you, your team, or your organization have an overwhelming goal or a dreaded job, make it into a game. Set small goals and give recognition when reaching benchmarks or completion. The game mindset brings enthusiasm, focus, and fun. Challenges become commonplace and no longer create negative stress. Utilize the game-positive-stress that keeps participants alert and performing at their best.

When playing a game by yourself, recognizing every small win will add to your feeling of satisfaction. Always celebrate success. Turning work into a game is the tool that has been instrumental in my positive attitude, energy, and success. It has worked for me, my teams and organizations. It will work for you and yours!

EVENTS, DESIRES, DREAMS
One step at a time to amazing success.

How old were you when you experienced an event that made a positive change in the direction of your life? I was nine years old when I experienced an event that would drastically change my life. Until then, I was a typical little girl growing up on a farm in rural southwest Iowa. The closest town was 10 miles—population 2,000 then and now. Like all rural children, I attended a one-room country school: one room, one teacher and all nine grades. The 'event' was the PTA meeting. It was exciting because after the business meeting there would be entertainment.

One night, a girl from town was the entertainment. She wore a white dress with a short skirt and white boots with tassels. As they introduced her a record started, a march. At that moment I saw a shiny silver stick in her hand. She moved it in beautiful circles, around, up and down, from hand to hand—so fast. She let go. It kept spinning—and she caught it! I couldn't believe it. How could anyone do that? It was so beautiful! They called it 'baton twirling.' If only I could do that. If I could just try. It became my dream.

What have you experienced in your life that was so special and wonderful it must not be real, it belongs only in a dream? And you want it so badly, you will do whatever is needed to get it? That's what my dream was. I wanted it so badly that I would do whatever was necessary to get it.

Making dreams into reality is difficult but extremely rewarding. It takes planning and working toward your goals. Focus on small goals just beyond your reach and never out of sight. It works! I set one little goal beyond my reach, reached it and set another. From a little goal, a step at a time, to escalating goals, escalating higher and higher. Before I knew it, my dream was a reality.

My dream was to become the World's Best Baton Twirler (always dream big!) and to win the National Championship. I didn't know there were over 20,000 other girls competing for the very same title. It is amazing what will come true if you want it badly enough, work hard enough, and are patient! It took me seven years to reach my goal and so well worth it.

I worked hard every day. *Every day* may sound too difficult but every day makes it easier because it becomes a habit. We all know habits are easy to do. Every day keeps us consistent and close to our goal. Be consistent and keep your goal specific and in clear vision.

You have only 24 hours every day. Set priorities for enough time and energy. The few sacrifices you must make will pale compared to the rewards.

I worked so hard and got the double baton twirl so fast, the basketball coach tied a blue nylon tarp rope to my right ankle to keep me from being airborne into the bleachers. No, but seriously, I worked very hard every day! If you work that hard in your field of endeavor, you will soar to great heights.

Dream BIG! Our dreams are what we visualize for the future, our creative visions of our future lives to be.

Never put limits on your potential. The higher you aim, the greater your possibilities. When you reach your high goal, aim higher. You and your team have more ability and untapped resources than you will ever know.

What is important to you? What is *most* important to you? Make a list and prioritize. The list will prepare you in how to live your life by keeping what you value most at the forefront, close to you and in clear vision.

I remember being on a little stage in Centerville, Iowa. It was opening ceremonies for the Annual Pancake Days. The chairman told me I was one of four people expected to say a few words. The other three were Mrs. America, First Runner-up to Miss America, and J. C. Penney—thee J. C. Penney—seated next to me. I was 17 years old and very nervous. I said to Mr. Penney, "I don't know what to say."

His blue eyes twinkled as he said, "That's easy, Honey, just talk about something important to you." He smiled, and I was introduced.

I don't remember exactly what I said except it was something important to me. It worked so well I'm still following Mr. Penney's advice—talking about and doing things important to me.

I have a question. Did you pursue that something so wonderful and special in your life? Or did you let it pass you by? It is never too late! If your desire is strong enough, it will motivate you with enough energy and patience to live your dreams with your eyes wide open.

- What events made positive changes in your life?
- Write about how they changed your life and give thanks.
- Which event changed the course of your life?
- Did you capitalize on it?

BELIEFS AND DESIRES
The power of beliefs and desires.

Have you ever thought about how we are human magnets? How we attract or draw to ourselves those things and people who respond to or are like our thoughts and our ideals? The scientific explanation is, all matter and energy vibrate as particles or rays. You attract to you whatever is similar in vibration. Your thoughts are energy and will attract the same kind of energy to you.

You become in life what you think about, talk about, attend to and feel deeply about.

"As a man thinketh in his heart so is he."
- **Proverbs 23:7 Thus, as a woman thinketh in her heart so is she.**

For centuries, world thought leaders have taught that desire is the inner motivation that keeps us moving forward in pursuit of our goals. This concept was presented in an audio program in 1950 by Earl Nightingale, called "The Strangest Secret." The secret being, 'You become what you think about.' That we are moved by our dominant thoughts, the thoughts we dwell on and think about most of the time.

Belief and desire release our abilities. My daughter spent the first four years of her life with me as I performed the opening act for the Harlem Globetrotters. When she was very young, she picked up a playground ball and spun it on her finger . . . for a long time. She was never taught how to spin a ball on her finger. She saw the Globetrotters spinning balls every night and assumed everyone could, so she just did it. Her belief and desire released the ability.

Many of us fail to reach our full potential because we assume we can't, so we don't even try. If we have not tested our strength, the strength of our abilities, how do we know what we are really capable of doing? Go after your dreams, believe you can achieve them . . . and you will amaze yourself.

What you believe is the key, or the barrier, to what you desire. Belief, as a positive force, is the fulfillment of what is hoped for and unseen. As a negative force, it is a premonition of your fears. Your belief determines your self-fulfilling prophecy, positive or negative. You are in charge of your control panel. Will you select negative and halting or positive and full-steam-ahead to what you desire?

What you expect to happen makes it happen. Your mind cannot distinguish between what is real and what is imagined. There is proof that many health issues are psychosomatic. The placebo effect, placebo meaning *I shall please* in Latin, has been proven, most times, to be as effective and longer lasting than actual medication. What you imagine, expect, and believe will happen becomes a reality.

I have found that good fortune is aided and supported by positive and grateful beliefs. Since I can remember, I have always said. "I'm so lucky!" If something bad happened, my response was, "So lucky it wasn't worse." Perhaps this belief stemmed from the snapshot I remember as a small child, my mother looking straight down at me and saying, "Joyce, you could fall into a mud puddle and come out clean!" It is all about perception.

My faith, my belief, has been paramount in my success, health, and happiness. My parents were my role models with their ability to do what needed done, no excuses, just do it. They had too much farm work to do to allow for sick time or self-doubt. They dealt with setbacks and never lost faith that tomorrow will be a new and better day. I have adopted their attitude, belief, and work ethic. The results are amazingly positive. However, allowing in negative thoughts and beliefs can quickly squelch the good fortune. Do not allow self-doubt, fears, any negative energy into your thoughts.

Negative thoughts deprive the body of endorphins, leading to depression and more negative thoughts. Positive thoughts and beliefs, and physical exercise create endorphins and a natural high. A natural endorphin high helps with nearly all discomforts: pain, stress, anxiety, depression, and so on. Why not be an endorphin junkie? You can be because you are in charge of your control panel!

The following is a true story confirming the power of the mind and the mind-body connection. What happened was not intentional and not a method I would advise others to follow.

My daughter and I, a comedy variety show known as Rice & Renee, were contracted to headline at a festival in Kansas. In fact, we were the only entertainment for the three-day event. The festival had spent their entire budget on Rice & Renee. We were to leave for Kansas on the next Tuesday. Friday, I suddenly became exhausted, having to lay down, sleep for a couple hours, get up and immediately having to repeat the sleep cycle. Saturday, I gained some energy and more on Sunday. I told my daughter, "I was just overly tired. I'll be fine to leave on Tuesday."

She replied, "Only after you go to the doctor Monday."

A long story short, I was hospitalized Monday and had a ball containing my burst appendix removed. The surprised surgeon said my immune system had formed a ball around the infected appendix by coating and encasing. My daughter took me home Tuesday morning and then drove with all the props to Kansas.

She performed solo for the children's show on Thursday and the campfire music on Friday. I flew in on Saturday and we, Rice & Renee, performed the Saturday night concert to a full house with a standing ovation.

After the nearly two-hour concert and signing autographs for another hour, I was totally exhausted. But what a great feeling of satisfaction! We had fulfilled our responsibility, the clients were extraordinarily pleased, and we could head home with time to recuperate.

When signing the contract, I had envisioned great success. Regardless of the nearly fatal barrier, we were given the strength needed to turn our vision into reality. I wanted to shout gratitude to my Creator. I opted for a passionate prayer of gratitude, "Thank you! Thank you! Thank you!"

SELF-WORTH & STRENGTHS
Assess, reset or build, and utilize.

We all are born with a clean slate and limitless potential, our true self. Talents and personality traits come naturally at birth.

Behavior patterns and habits are learned through observation, imitation, and repetition. All we learn adds to, or smothers, our true self. We learn by imitating those around us, how they act, what they say, and what they do. Our belief system, our identity, our character traits are formed and rooted by our relationships and environment.

If you have self-limiting beliefs of helplessness, hopelessness or worthlessness, the good news is that you can reset. New thinking and training can dissolve self-limiting beliefs and dismiss blame on external people and circumstances. External conditions can slow you but not stop you. Surround yourself with positive people who support your success. Their belief in you rejuvenates your confidence and true self-capabilities.

You are in control of how others treat you. You teach them by being true to yourself or giving up your power.

"There are no victims in this world, only volunteers. If you really want a change in your relationships or in any area of your life, you must acknowledge that you alone have chosen your experience through both your attitude and actions."
-Dr. Phil McGraw

Tap into your true self. Listen to your heart and instincts. During quiet time, in complete silence with no distractions:

- List all the Life Lessons you experienced.

- Divide the list into two columns, Good and Bad.

- Beside each Life Lesson, write what you learned. You will find some Bad were beneficial in your growth.

- Again, divide the Bad into two columns, Strengthening and Erased.

- The Life Lessons under the Erased column, do just that, erase from the page and your thoughts. Holding on to negativity gives it strength. Keep the Strengthening Bad in the back of your mind and use only for red-flagging similar experiences in the future.

Assess the talents and attributes you were born with and those you built on because of your interest and love. Winners know who they are and where they are. They have a vision and plans for tomorrow. Knowing your attributes, abilities, interests, strengths, weaknesses, and traits is essential to becoming proactive in building or changing a career.

Unlike twirlers in world-class competition, I didn't have dance training. I couldn't toss a baton in the air, turn around six times and catch the baton behind my back. But I could toss a baton 60 feet in the air and catch it. I was fearless and strong. I had grown up milking cows by hand. My forearms and hands were strong, very important for twirling. The added strength increased my control, precision, and smoothness, giving me an advantage.

Always rely and build on your strengths. Your abilities are as unique as your fingerprints, use them. In a copycat world of those watching videos and replicating, being unique is a breath of fresh air and guarantees being seen.

Whip cracking requires back strength. When I started, only men did whip acts. They had the strength to hold a 12-foot whip in one hand and do repetitive cracks. I couldn't. So, I would turn sideways to the audience, hold the 12-foot whip in both hands over my head and crack it to my front and back while doing a backbend.

It began as something I couldn't do. By adapting it to what I could do, it became my signature and ending trick: doing my overhead two-handed repetitive cracks in a backbend, suddenly standing straight, pointing to a rose and snapping it out of the vase on my prop table. It was extraordinary because it was unique.

The funniest video I saw of a copycat was of a very buffed-out Mr. Universe type with his hands over his head and leaning slightly to the back. He didn't realize why I used two hands or how it did not fit him. Watching others can initiate ideas that can be used with your style and ability. Never copy. You may end up appearing very foolish.

We all have our 'if-only dream worlds.' Always aim high and dream big! Our imagination quotient is of greater value than our intelligence quotient.

> *"Imagination is more important than knowledge. Knowledge is limited. Imagination encircles the world."*
> -Albert Einstein

Who you think and imagine you are governs your actions and destiny. Your greatest limitations are those you put on yourself. Rewrite your limitation script and set yourself free. Unlock the chains of limitations and claim victory!

You hold the keys to being and getting what you want. There are no unrealistic goals, just unrealistic time frames.

> *"Rome wasn't built in a day, but they were laying bricks every hour."*
> -attributed to John Heywood, an English writer known for his plays, poems, and collection of proverbs. He lived from 1497–1540.

ATTITUDE
You control your attitude as it controls your life.

Attitude is paramount! It is at the uppermost pinnacle and trickles down *or* floods your entire life. Your attitude is all-encompassing, affecting every area of your life. As previously written, it determines the level of your potential, produces the intensity of your activity, and predicts the quality of the result you receive. A positive attitude is mandatory for your success, personally and professionally, for your happiness, and for your health. Positive attracts positive! Negative attracts negative.

Nothing and no other person is responsible for your attitude. You are, only you. You decide between being happy or sad, victor or victim, grateful or blaming, on and on. If your attitude falls into the negative, take action to improve it. You can't control what life hands you, but you can control how you react to life's circumstances.

Attending Iowa State on a full scholarship was a dream come true. I even had the perfect roommate, except she was gloom and doom for an hour every morning. What if, instead, she were expectant and joyful for her many opportunities every hour of the day? So, every morning, as soon as I saw she was awake, I'd raise up the blind and sing, "Oh, what a beautiful morning, oh, what a beautiful day. I've got a wonderful feeling everything's going our way." Rain or snow didn't change the tune or improve my singing. During the first year of our four years rooming together, she became bright and chipper in the morning, *or* she faked it to keep me from singing.

My roommate's gloomy attitude for the first hour of her day was a habit. Experts say a negative attitude or habit can change by replacing it with a positive habit, but it takes work and time. My horrible singing wasn't hard nor did it take much time to make a win for her and a win for me. Developing and maintaining a positive attitude mindset enhances your life and all you touch.

As Martha Washington said in 1789,

"I am determined to be cheerful and to be happy, in whatever situation I may be; for I have also learnt, from experience, that the greater part of our happiness or misery depends upon our dispositions, and not upon our circumstances."

We all have inspiring people in our lives, sometimes we need to be reminded. My little hometown had two remarkable men. They inspired everyone with their joyful can-do attitudes.

Al contracted polio as a young teenager. His treatment was the grueling Iron Lung. He felt lucky, lucky to have survived and able to go fishing and have a thriving shoe repair business. The polio had paralyzed his legs, so he built a track in his long narrow shop and attached a chair. With the strength of his arms, his chair could glide over the track to his equipment and tables needed for his work. He was quick, efficient, did excellent work, and with a smile. When any shoe repair needed done, I always wanted to take them to Al. Seeing him was a joy. Opening the door to Al's Shoe Repair was like opening a door to happiness and sunshine. He made everyone feel they were a gift of sunshine. In reality, his positive attitude was the sunshine and never to be forgotten.

Gil was an energetic high school student. He loved leading his dance band throughout the state at many current and recurring engagements. During his senior year, his physical problems were diagnosed as the beginning of a progressive and fatal rare disease. Loading equipment in and out of engagements became impossible for him so he turned to teaching young aspiring musicians and opened a music store. From a small rural area came an abundance of budding musicians, more than the whole state, claiming Gil as their inspiration, mentor and friend. They became professional musicians in many national bands, music directors and professors of music.

To provide the needed income for himself and his parents, Gil expanded his music store. When he had no mobility, his elderly parents were his legs. His parents passed away and his health was rapidly declining. His only choice in sitting was being placed in a leaning position in an easy chair with wheels giving him a sense of mobility. With hands so crippled he could no longer open the cash register and with customers having to make their own change, Gil developed a new purpose; being the information center for those looking for work and those needing workers. Every day Gil, the most positive and inspiring person I have ever known, moved a toggle switch on his desk at exactly 12 o'clock noon, activating the noon whistle in the little town. Never did I hear him complain, but rather saying, "Tomorrow will be a good day." He was thankful to be alive and able to contribute.

A positive attitude makes the impossible possible!

The hayfield of red clover filled my senses and my spirit with thankfulness to experience the wonders of nature. A noonday sun highlighted the red flowers and intensified the sweet clover-smell interspersed with the buzzing of bees busy with pollination. I noticed him. He was bigger, slower, never losing focus. With his yellow stripes and bulky body, he was fulfilling his purpose. The bumblebee didn't know he could not fly, so he did. And I didn't hear him voice one complaint!

> *"Look deep into nature and then you will understand everything better."*
>
> - Albert Einstein

PREPARATION/COURAGE/CONFIDENCE

Preparation leads.

My brother used to call me Fido. We had only one bicycle, so he'd ride the bicycle and I'd be the dog. Yes, he was an older brother. He also called me Diz after the baseball great Dizzy Dean. He was the catcher on our school's softball team, and when he wanted to practice his catching, I would have to pitch.

It was in the spring of my fourth-grade year at Grand River #2 country school. We were playing a game of softball against Grand River #4. My brother, a sixth grader, was the catcher. Me, I was right field. I was a good pitcher. Anyway, that's what my brother told me when he wanted to practice his catching. He'd squat down into the pro position, hit his mitt and say, "Right here, Diz, right here." He called me quite a few names but Diz was one of my favorites.

Back to the ballgame. Our arch rival was winning! What if a ball came to right field, and I dropped it? It is scary being one of the little kids. Then I saw the big boys holding a conference, they looked straight at me. The pitcher was upset. He was a seventh grader. Next thing I knew, I was on the pitcher's mound which was actually just a bare spot in the grass.

My brother squatted down behind the batter and hit his mitt just like he always did. It was quiet, really quiet, except for my pounding heart. My eyes zeroed in on my brother's mitt, I shifted my weight back, stepped forward and let it go. Strike one! Everyone was surprised, except maybe my brother. He acted like it was a common occurrence. And me, well, down deep, real deep, I thought I could do it. I had thrown a fastball into that mitt hundreds of times.

We struck out the first batter, the second batter got on first base, struck out the third and caught the fourth's fly ball. No runs! We made some runs. The next inning, I pitched again and only one run. We got ahead. The big boy pitcher came back in and we won! I'd had my day in the sun. Under pressure, I had done it. My brother said, "Aw, Diz, you'd done it so many times."

Yes, I had thrown a ball into my brother's mitt so many times—I was prepared! But preparation had given me more than skill; it had given me the courage to accept the opportunity—and the confidence to win. The greatest builder of confidence and courage is preparation!

It makes sense knowing the word *confidence* is derived from the Latin word 'confidere' meaning trust. Only through preparation do you grow to trust your ability and have confidence in your ability and yourself. The greatest builder of your confidence and courage is what? Preparation!

Abraham Lincoln, the 16th President of the United States, as a young man wrote,

"I shall prepare and prepare and prepare and when my time comes, I will be ready."

If you prepare and prepare and prepare, when your time comes, you will be ready!

Section Two

WORK IT!

CHARTING YOUR COURSE

Assess Who, What, Where with clarity, enthusiasm, and patience.

If you are indecisive about who you are, who are you not? It is easy to know who you are not.

1. Divide a paper into two columns. Write **who you are not** in the first column. During the exercise, you will discover a degree of distaste for who you are not, and it will become clear who you are by elimination.

2. On the second column write **who you are.**

3. Do the same exercise with **what you want** and **what you don't want.**

Knowing, and having written on paper, who you are and what you want gives grounding and clarity. Observe what you don't want. Study what you do want.

Before mapping a course of action, **know where you are**. Knowing how to reach your destination is impossible without knowing the starting point. You can quickly state your physical location, but where are you **regarding financial resources, health, desire, aptitude, mindset**?

1. List all the factors on the left side of the page and the assessment of each on the right side. By having them on paper, rather than trying to do the impossible feat of keeping everything in your brain, organized and prioritized, you can plan strategically.

2. Look at each factor where you are starting from, and improvement needed to reach your desired destination.

3. What can you do?

4. Who can help?

5. Prioritize the factors as to importance in reaching your goal.

6. Which will be the easiest and fastest to improve and use as leverage on your route to success?

7. Chart your course and take action.

To prevent being overwhelmed, keep your sheets available and course updated. Compare where you are now to where you started. Realize your improvement and visualize where you are going. Keep your goals specific and in clear view. Be consistent in improving every day. A step a day compounds into a giant leap.

Do the best you can, with what you have, where you are. You will find everything else you need will gradually become available. There is no instant in any worthwhile goal.

It seemed strange when I first noticed how working to improve any one thing improved everything else. It is true and why you must constantly challenge yourself, focus on improvement. 'Divine discontent' moves you forward. Complacency is death to progress.

I'll never forget the first time I tried to twirl a baton. My family had gone to visit the neighbors. After supper, the neighbor girl showed me what she had gotten from the Sears, Roebuck, and Company mail-order catalog. A baton! I was so excited. It was beautiful. Shiny silver steel with rubber ends. It was very long. She held on to the center of the baton and turned it so one end of the baton went on the inside of her arm and the other end went on the outside or elbow side of her arm. That's what the diagram had.

All the children tried it, but I couldn't stop. I was still trying hours later when it was time to go home. My arm and shoulder felt weak, my hand was red from constant use, but it was my elbow that really hurt. It was red and swollen and had begun to turn black. The inside of my arm, my ribs, my leg were black and blue. What a mess I was for having so much fun. I really wanted to twirl that baton. There was no limit to my desire!

But that was only the beginning. Words can't express my joy when I got my first baton and went to my first lesson. My teacher was the girl I had seen perform at the PTA meeting. She was going to teach me what I wanted to do more than anything.

I was excited and afraid. What if I couldn't do it? What if I couldn't remember? Before I went home, I wrote down what I had learned. Wrist twirl right hand and left hand. It was the twirl I had tried to do that evening at the neighbor's. Every day I practiced. Every two weeks I learned another twirl. Now I had the explanation and understanding to go with my goal and motivation, which eliminated the frustration.

There was no limit to my enthusiasm! Many say enthusiasm is the secret to success. I agree enthusiasm ranks right along the top, but it needs to be consistent which can be difficult. Don't allow others to rain on your enthusiasm. Consider their knowledge and motive. If neither is positive, keep doing what is a positive benefit to you and those you love.

> *"Knowledge is power,*
> *but enthusiasm pulls the switch."*
>
> \- Ivern Bell

Never let enthusiasm squelch patience. Both need to be strong and consistent. It takes time to turn life-changing visions and goals into reality. However, time flies when you are doing what you love!

TIME
Investing or spending?

There is no such thing as time management. Time is a finite asset. There are 24 hours in a day, no more, no less. The only thing you can manage is what you do with the allotted time. You choose how to use your time.

- Spending time for consumption - How much time are you spending on entertainment, on what attracts you at the moment or beckons from afar?

- Investing time for growth - How much time are you investing in activities that will grow your health, knowledge, relationships, skills, and money for future use?

Few people are willing to invest one hour a day in themselves to reach their full potential. They have the potential but not the discipline. Will you use one hour of time daily to focus on getting better at what you love to do? Practice and hone your skills.

I have three longtime friends who are internationally acclaimed the "Best" in their professions—all different professions and personalities, but all three are the same in their enthusiasm for life and their ease in accomplishing very difficult tasks and trials. They invested time building and working at what they loved. Their response to age is also the same,

> *"Yes, I'd like to be young again, not to change anything that has happened in my life, only to have more time. There is still so much to do with so little time."*

Time cannot be replaced. How you choose to use time determines opportunity, cost and results received. Be cautious about where and how much time you spend. Is there enough time left to invest in your future? Plan on paper a rough estimate of the time necessary for you to invest in learning and preparing skills needed to reach your goal. Update and prioritize regularly. In all areas of your life, balancing time spent and time invested is your choice.

Never let things that matter the least get in the way of those things that matter the most. Use your time and energy wisely. List four people, four activities, four foods or drinks that sap your time and energy. They are draining your fountains. Walk away from the drains and replenish your fountains. Getting to a better place requires that you raise your standards and say "No" to the drains. Free time allows time for fulfilling conversations and activities to grow and serve.

Keep true to your vision and use time wisely. Time used for investing will compound interest for you and those you love.

BASICS
All is built on them.

Preparation is key. When preparing, remember the importance of mastering the basics. In any field of endeavor, perfect the basics! Unfortunately, in our fast-paced lives, basics are often rushed over, if not eliminated. There is no shortcut. The height of your success will be determined by how well you master the basics.

My first baton teacher taught me all she knew, the basics and a few variations. Since I had only a few twirls to concentrate on, they became very good. When I had the opportunity to learn the fancy twirls, there was no stopping me because all twirls are made from the basics.

In all things a beginner is slow and deliberate, you should be. If you can't do it slowly, you can't do it fast!

The first twirl I learned was a full-hand basic called the wrist twirl. This was the twirl I had desperately tried and failed to do while visiting the neighbors. When I first learned the wrist twirl, I was jerky and stiff. As a beginner, we are afraid and hold on too tightly. That's true in everything—

speaking, management, leading. Once we learn, we relax and guide rather than restrain.

A baton is only a baton. Spinning a baton is really nothing until you can make it spin so fast you can't see it, then you have something.

In whatever area you wish to excel, keep honing and improving the basics, all is built on them. They are the foundation and the building blocks of your one-story or skyscraper. Once you perfect the basics, you can develop a program. Create, innovate, whatever you'd like because you have the foundation and building blocks, opening a world of possibilities.

Apply the principle of perfected basics to your chosen field of endeavor. You will experience how a solid foundation with building blocks gives you the needed stability and confidence for rapid and consistent success.

RISKS
Embrace risks.

Those who risk nothing avoid failure and any opportunity for success.

There is nothing without risks. Risks must be taken. Not risking is the greatest hazard in life. Only a person who risks is totally free, free to learn, feel, change, grow, love and live. Are you willing to risk what you have for what you are capable of?

My best friend laughed at me and told me I was incapable of getting in the band. It is important to remember when a friend turns against you, to think for yourself and not let hurtful comments deter your progress. It is important to share feelings with a confidant so they can comfort and support you.

The phrase my mother told me, "You do what *you* think is right and don't worry about what others say," has saved me from many disparaging issues. When you apply that phrase to your life, it will empower you five-fold. You won't allow others to intimidate you or devalue your dream, you will trust yourself to know and do the right thing, and you will accept responsibility and focus on your desired goal.

Never focus or dwell on possible setbacks. Losers dwell on the penalties of failure; winners dwell on the rewards of success. Only by risking are you totally free.

My grandmother was a sweet, kind lady. She was pretty with big blue eyes, wavy pure white hair, straight posture, and a quick step. Everyone loved her and she wanted the same for me.

I used the money I made raising ducks to pay tuition for eighth grade in town school, making me eligible to audition for twirler in the high school band. Shortly after I accomplished my first goal of becoming a twirler in the high school band, Grandma said, "Joyce, I am very proud of you, but you are good enough. If you get better, people won't like you as much."

I didn't understand how she was trying to protect me. I learned! When you change or rise above mediocrity, there may be jealousy or feelings of abandonment from those left behind.

Even though I do not equate humans with crabs, the story I'm about to tell you relates to human nature.

A bucket with a few inches of water in the bottom contains variously sized crabs. There is one ambitious little crab climbing on top of other crabs trying to gain height, so he can grab the rim of the bucket and escape to freedom. Just as he gains height to reach the top and pull himself over the edge of the bucket, the other crabs reach up, grab his hind legs and pull him down to the bottom of the bucket.

Allowing people to pull you down hurts you and them. Eliminate the negative crabs. Surround yourself with supportive, positive and like-value people. Once you succeed in reaching your dream through persistence and staying true to yourself, even the negative crabs will be inspired. You will have grown and inspired countless others.

Will you take the risk of claiming the dreams within you?

CONCENTRATE AND RELAX
Key to learning and performing

A friend, a former champion steer roper turned actor, told me that the most important prerequisite to learning or performing a task is being able to concentrate and relax at the same time. He is right, and it is easier said than done. Concentration and relaxation at the same time are vital to learning and performing a task well.

When spinning a rope, you must concentrate to do it, but also relax because rope spinning is all timing and you must feel. Relax and Feel. Guide, but don't force. As with most everything—especially relationships—work hard and let it flow, with gentle guidance.

In a restaurant, I saw a picture of a little cowboy with oversized boots and a hat, swinging a big lasso. The caption read, 'A slow loop and a gentle hand will catch a lot of happiness from each day upon this land.' Relax and feel.

To make a point to his officers, General and President of the United States, Dwight Eisenhower would lay a piece of rope on the table and ask, "Which is the most efficient way to move this rope, push or pull?" A rope may be very strong, but it cannot be pushed to a target with any degree of accuracy. It only follows your guidance. You, as parents or managers or even presidents of the United States, you don't push people to greatness—you *pull* them—you inspire and lead them!

Of the three skills I developed to 'master level,' rope spinning was my least favorite. With all the baton adaptations, it was unique, but it tried my patience. It could not stand on its own. I had to guide every move. It only followed. Every day, it was different. Ropes absorb moisture so humidity affects how limp or how stiff a rope is and can quickly change. Television studios are difficult because they're humid with very hot lights.

Rope spinning requires relaxing and feeling, important abilities for life. I was constantly adapting and guiding by feeling. The rope is attached and only follows. I was responsible for every mistake it made! It demanded patience.

Baton twirling and whip cracking are invigorating. Batons are shiny and whips are loud. They attract attention and require attention. The spring steel baton can break bones and the whip can put a deep burn on bare skin.

Inanimate objects can teach powerful life lessons. The challenge is getting them to do what you want. You have full ownership of the outcome.

We know people and experience situations with attributes similar to the rope, baton, and whip. Therefore, it is important to know what we want and mandatory that we are flexible and adjust.

VISUALIZATION
More than a mind's eye vision of dreams, actions, and outcomes.

Visualization is a powerful tool in achieving positive outcomes. By using the latest advancements in neuroscience, modern psychology can help you visualize goals into action and accomplish your goals and dreams. Take the time to create a clear image for your mind to focus on and turn your idea into a vision that can move you forward with certainty.

I was introduced to a practice called 'Cognitive Priming' by John Assaraf, a brain science expert, best-selling author, and founder of NeuroGym. 'Cognitive Priming' helps stimulate new, positive neural pathways in the brain. The following steps help create a clear, concrete image of what you want to accomplish.

1. Take 10–15 minutes and write a goal, big or small. Be detailed in your description and as clear as possible. By doing this, you are activating your visual cortex.

2. Review what you wrote. Impress all the details into your mind. How does it feel, look, smell? This will prime your brain for action. You'll notice your thoughts, feelings, and emotions will change ... and your behavior will begin aligning with the goal, setting you on a path toward success.

3. Imagine what it feels like after you achieve your goal.

This is cognitive priming, and it stimulates the "genius" part of your brain located in the prefrontal cortex. Practicing creative visualization is a way to train your brain for success. By learning how to retrain your brain, you'll fulfill more of what you are capable of achieving, elevating your potential.

Visualization plays a major role in my life. In fact, can anything happen without it? From creating to completing, nothing makes me hustle more than visualizing how good my competitors are. They serve as a measure of competence for me to reach.

Have you ever gone from being the big duck in a little pond to being a little duck in the big pond? I have. I became invisible in the big pond.

There wasn't money for more than an occasional lesson from a baton teacher in Des Moines and a week at a twirling camp in Indiana. Everything I learned I perfected and put in my routine, the routine I performed at the State Championship Contest. Since it was Iowa's first state competition and few contestants, I won first place, qualifying me to enter the National Championship Contest held at St. Paul, Minnesota.

The local Lions Club sponsored me. Little did we know, compared to other twirlers throughout the United States and

Canada, I was a mere beginner. The other contestants at the national competition varied in ability—from good to unbelievably great! It was plain to see, I was far, very far, behind. But, instead of feeling invisible and defeated, I was inspired and motivated. I had seen excellence. That is where I wanted to be. I decided to practice twice as hard as all the other twirlers so I could catch up to them. It was the beginning of my Can-Do Plan: Think it, Work it, Do it!

Every morning I visualized them practicing and performing their beautiful routines, motivating me to practice, practicing every day and challenging myself to be better than yesterday. I visualized how it would be, with the others, on top of the mountain.

Visualize being, doing and having what you want. Take action every day to move forward toward your vision.

> *"To believe in the things you can see and touch is no belief at all, but to believe in the unseen is both triumph and a blessing."*
>
> -Abraham Lincoln

VALUE OF LOSING
A win in learning.

Losing is seldom a lesson that parents teach their children. They push for 'the win.' When a loss occurs, everyone becomes overly emotional. Learning halts. Most people quit and never experience their wins in losing.

Losing is a reality check. It keeps you humble and challenged to improve next time OR move on to what is a better fit. I'm not saying quit and change directions after your first few losses, only after carefully assessing your aptitude and what you desire. Without testing your ability in varied positions and disciplines, how can you know what you like and where your talents lie?

In all of life, it is *win or learn*. Toss out losses and look ahead to victory. Those shedding the fear of loss become fearless and free to embrace change and, of major importance, be authentic with unwavering integrity.

I credit attending a one-room country school as a huge blessing on my road to maturity and success. That was where

I learned that losing was neither fatal nor forever, and instant gratification was never available.

With only one teacher and all nine grades, there was little attention given to individual students. I learned very young, I was responsible for achieving what I wanted. It was up to me! Yes, I was a loser more often than a winner. In kindergarten, I was always the worst in everything but learned that next year I'd do better. With each additional year, I lost less and increased empathy for those younger. Having more wins than losses was not an overnight gift.

There were very few people in that little school. I could not discard those I didn't like. I must get along and work with everyone. Every day of the eight years I attended that country school, I was stretching mentally and physically. I was challenged by seeing those farther down the road and learned to be tolerant of those just beginning. The 'real world' of wins and losses was mine to experience.

There were many distractions in that one-room school, from the teacher having a class discuss their lesson at the front of the room, to a little kid sitting near me silently eating paste! Learning to concentrate and focus was vital.

During recess, I learned to run fast and play my best. I didn't like being the last kid picked on a team. What I learned (of great value and used throughout life) were the tools needed to excel in any field of choice.

Tools such as:

- being responsible, patient, persistent, consistent
- developing the ability to focus and concentrate
- having empathy, hope, vision

- experiencing and valuing cooperation, teamwork, leadership

- doing the best of my ability

You and I possess all the listed tools in varying degrees. We instinctively know which need improvement. All are important and have room for improvement. Why bother? Because, they work synergistically in attaining optimal results, personally and professionally.

Your road to success can begin with two words: saying 'I can' gives you emotional freedom to proceed. Proceeding leads to a determined 'I will.' Emotional freedom and determination lead to 'I did!' and the ultimate reward: satisfaction of accomplishment.

Completion hinges on your determination. You are wealthy if you have determination or any one of its synonyms; perseverance, persistence or tenacity. Your wealth lies in your determination and accumulation of useful tools needed to reach your goals.

MENTORS
Precious and life-changing

The Merriam-Webster dictionary defines a mentor as a trusted counselor or guide, a tutor or coach.

Be open to mentoring at every stage of your life and career. Perspectives vary in value. Assess, adapt or disregard and always, always learn. Two brief comments, one given in support and one given in envy, made a huge difference in my life and why I consider both as mentoring.

Kate was a trusted guide, a retired schoolteacher who never retired from teaching children. I was my brother's younger sister, the little tag-along. We would walk up the dirt road to visit our closest neighbor, Kate. She always had a learning project. This day, it was weighing a lamb.

When we arrived, we saw a lamb in a small chicken-wire fence in the front yard. Next to the pen was a large scale. Kate came out of the house. She greeted us and said, "Today we are going to weigh the lamb. How should we do it?"

I have no idea what I said, but I will always remember how Kate made me feel. She placed her hand on top of my head, a four-year-old's head who always felt dumb in comparison, and said, "Joyce, that is right. You are very smart."

With those few words, Kate had given me a moment of feeling smart, an exhilarating feeling of worth. She had lit a spark within me. A spark that squelched feeling dumb to opening the door to valedictorian and scholastic honors. Giving a small child words of encouragement is giving the child a lifetime gift.

My best friend nearly killed my dream of being a twirler in the high school band by scoffing and saying, "You can't do that! They are good." My mother saved the day when she said "You do what you think is right. Don't worry about what others say."

The negative comment, from whom I thought was a friend, gave me added resolve to reach my goal. I learned my parents trusted me to know what is right, and it was my responsibility to disregard negative comments. Three slam-dunks in a row!

Two-sentence or lifetime mentoring may appear anywhere, anytime—and change your life. Be grateful for parents, teachers, and supporters giving guidance and inspiration to bring out your best, by telling you to never give up, and by being caring and comforting.

The first baton twirler I saw inspired me, she became my teacher/mentor. Her expertise was the baton basics. She performed them perfectly and expected the same from her students. I can still picture her baton spinning so fast and effortlessly. She was my role model.

In any field of endeavor, your first teacher is the most important. Seek out the Best. They are the ones who know the importance of the basics. To make sure you didn't miss why perfecting the basics is so important, I'll repeat: "The basics are the foundation and building blocks of your one-story or skyscraper. All is built on them."

Aim for the top. Aim to be the best! To be the best in the world, you have to say it. However, be selective to whom you say it. Those not understanding the importance will call you narcissistic or worse. However, without aspirations of being the best and saying it, your brain doesn't know its direction. Your brain doesn't understand second best or mediocre.

Truthfully, I never said it out loud until the state competition judge asked me. He saw my poorly constructed routine. After the competition, he sought me out and asked, "How far do you want to go?"

I bravely replied, "I want to be the best." He smiled and offered to reconstruct my routine, free of charge! I accepted!

It was three days of the most intensive building and learning I had ever experienced. He reconstructed my routine while teaching me the 'how to' of superior routine construction. I returned home mentally and physically exhausted, but could not have been more grateful! I had been given the vehicle and know-how that could take me and my baton students to the top. The responsibility for practicing and perfecting was up to me. I joyously accepted!

The second time I competed at the National, equipped with a properly constructed routine and hundreds of practice hours, I was no longer invisible. I placed somewhere in the top 20. The following year I placed fifth. On my fourth try, when I was 17 years old, I won the National Baton Twirling Championship and was named 'Best in the World.'

My mentor, who so generously shared his expertise, gave me the vehicle that could reach the top. He was the best in the world in routine structuring and worked with many champions throughout the country. I was only one of many. It was my good fortune that he offered to help me. He would never have helped me had I said I wanted to be mediocre.

Be grateful to your Creator and those who teach, inspire and support you—all great mentors know when and how to lead. The help we need is often very near. All that is required of us is being open to accepting and utilizing the help.

INNOVATION
The secret to success.

I must have been born with innovation at the forefront of my thinking. Looking for ways of improvement and experiencing improvement is what fulfills me. My first memory of trying new ways to improve was while sitting on top of a wagonload of ear corn.

My chore was to throw a certain number of ears over the fence to the hogs. I made a game out of different ways to throw the ears and which were best. I got my job done and had fun challenging myself to find different and better ways.

Throwing ears of corn over a fence is menial and repetitious unless you pay attention to the details. Just as a beach is the color and texture of its grains of sand, in whatever you wish to accomplish, it is the details that can turn mediocre into exceptional.

Two days after winning the national championship and being named "Best in the World," I was in New York City for a TV appearance when I was told, "Today's headlines fill tomorrow's Trash Cans." It made me realize, there is no time to rest on laurels. The rest of the world keeps moving.

I decided to not let winning be the end, but rather a stepping stone on my journey. I took what I already knew, kept improving it and adapting it to other disciplines. By doing that, I created more than ever. You do the same and you'll have the same outcome! Take what you already know, keep improving it and adapting it to other disciplines. You too will create more and more. As Oliver Wendell Holmes said,

> *"Man's mind once stretched by a new idea never regains its original dimensions."*

Baton twirling is like everything else in life, you get out of it what you put into it. To be good, it takes work. To be the best it takes devotion. Maintaining the #1 position takes work, devotion, and unrelenting innovation. Innovation in the basics or key ingredients determines your continuing success. In sales, management, family living or studies, the very same principles apply.

Success is fragile. You never own success. You can only rent it. Assess what made the success. Are you still doing that as aggressively and consistently? Are you innovating and improving? You cannot stand still. You are moving forward or backward. As Will Rogers said,

> *"Even if you are on the right track, you'll get run over if you sit there."*

Rogers is my hero because he personifies the best as a creator, innovator, and man of action. He capitalized on humor with his folksy wit and common-sense attitude. Writing more than 4,000 nationally syndicated newspaper columns, traveling around the world three times as an entertainer and humorist, and making 71 films, Rogers was one of the most popular stars of the 1920s and 30s. There was no better man of action, all the while with a twinkle of enthusiasm in his eyes and a smile on his lips. His life was cut short by his untimely death at age 55.

Innovation is assessing, adapting and implementing. It is usually based on the convergence of several kinds of knowledge. The Wright brothers developed their airplane using the gasoline motor powering the first automobiles and the mathematics of aerodynamics, developed in experiments with gliders. Each knowledge was developed independently. By converging the two, the airplane became possible. What do you already know that can be combined or adapted to a new skill or knowledge you acquire?

Innovating has been fun and very valuable for me. I had a successful career as a baton/juggling act. Not only did I work at improving my presentation but I also did not take the easy route of—"The audience won't know the difference."

Audiences and clients may not know the difficulty of your expertise, but they see and feel your commitment and passion. Emotions are energy with vibrations that are transmitted. I respected the audience and never gave them the easy, watered-down version of my presentation. I performed worldwide because I kept growing and giving 100% effort to my audiences.

The journey is what is exciting! Keep your eyes open. Some of the best things may come at unexpected times and places.

It was North Platte, Nebraska, 20 years after I had seen the baton twirler who changed my life. I had traveled nearly all over the world performing a baton/juggling act. I was married with a 6-year-old daughter when it happened again—that same fascination, quickening of the pulse, and feeling of 'I have to learn how to do it.'

I would adapt all the baton knowledge and skill into my new obsession with becoming the world's best (always aim high) and most unique multiple cracking whip artist. It's true. I had just seen one of the best. He was from Australia. It was beautiful. It reminded me of spinning batons with firecrackers on the ends.

I hate violence and loud noises. So, it would be a huge challenge to make whip cracking a pretty art. I had seen a vision. I must make it a reality!

My first step: Find a teacher to teach me the whip basics and technique. I found him living in Chicago, an 80-year-old vaudevillian named Bud Carlell. He was a big man from Oklahoma, stern and willing to help me. He had worked venues from rodeos to big stages with the greats. A few were Tom Mix, Will Rogers, and Mitzi Gaynor.

My first lesson was in a large room on the top floor of the retirement hotel where he lived. Taking the coiled whips from his prop satchel, he cracked a 12-foot kangaroo hide whip from corner to corner. It looked like a black snake and sounded like a shotgun. It took my breath away. I wasn't sure which emotion was the strongest, amazement or fright. I could see he was the absolute best, being a perfectionist with 65 years of experience. To make whip cracking a pretty art would be a huge challenge!

Bud taught me the whip basics and safety tips. He introduced me to the two basic kinds, bullwhips and stock whips, and where to buy shorter whips to suit what I had in mind. When he realized I was afraid of the whips (the sound is due to breaking the sound barrier), he taught me rope spinning.

I purchased two short whips and gained the courage to develop a whip routine. Using my baton knowledge and stage experience, and with Bud's coaching, I developed a unique whip cracking act that audiences applauded.

Because I believed with all my heart, *"Do what you think is right and don't worry about what others say."* I learned how to crack a whip and perform it. A few years later, I became a sought-after professional, again performing worldwide and this time being featured on many national and international television shows.

My style of whip cracking was unique and so was my demeanor—smiling and friendly in place of threatening and dangerous. My daughter would say, "Mom is Betty Crocker with Whips!" Working many overseas engagements, I became known as 'America's Favorite Cowgirl.'

I added audience participation, showing skill and comedy. Traditional circus enthusiasts complained when I used audience participation. It later became commonplace in the circus and on stage.

The hilarious audience participation with the whips endeared the participant to all watching. He would be blindfolded, bent over with a handkerchief in his hip pocket. I would then put a hood over my head and snap out the handkerchief with the cracking whip. The participant was showcased as a good sport and favorable personality. I worked with many politicians, law enforcement officials and television hosts looking for fun, positive public relations.

My favorite participants on television shows and why: Dom DeLuise was the most selfless and fun, Don Rickles was kind and the wildest, Maury Povich was the most hospitable, and the grandest gentleman telegraphing complete confidence in the guest was Mike Douglas.

If I hadn't kept innovating and evolving, I would have missed many opportunities and so much enjoyment. My innovation concept is, 'The deliberate process of enhancing or improving the relevant perceived value of a product, a service, or even a company as determined by a specifically predefined marketplace . . . capitalizing on the attributes of change as a valuable ally.'

My How-to Incremental Innovation Concept involves six steps.

1. Define the top 10 most critical elements influencing success in your business or profession.

2. Rearrange these elements in the most logical chronological sequence.

3. Identify a recognizable role model or point of reference for each of these elements.

4. Rate your overall level of effectiveness at each of the elements using a scale of 1–10. (Consider margin for improvement.)

5. Dissect each element down into its key ingredients.

6. Determine the actions needed to improve or enhance each key ingredient of all the elements by priority.

Steve Jobs was one of the most profitable innovators. He took existing ideas and products, improved, updated and repackaged them for current times. He borrowed ideas and products that already worked and improved them!

Take what you know, keep learning, creating, innovating, and use as stepping stones to your next milestone.

Like fingerprints, we differ from one another. Use your uniqueness. The original is always better than the carbon copy. You are the best there is at being you, producing what you do best, in your way. Don't be afraid to be yourself. Let your uniqueness show. Your uniqueness will no doubt be your catapult to success.

I remember being apprehensive about going to work in Saudi Arabia but also very excited. It was a long trip from Chicago with some problems at immigration. When I arrived at my new home for the next three weeks, I quickly fell asleep in the very foreign land.

I awakened at dawn by the singing of a bird—the most beautiful sounds I had ever heard, so sweet and melodious. Every morning the beautiful singing awakened me. I became very curious what this bird looked like. The next morning, I got up at dawn, determined to find the bird with those beautiful songs. I spotted him with head thrown back, singing for all he was worth—a mousy gray, nondescript bird.

After a brief feeling of disappointment, I thought, how true to life. Every creature on earth has its own kind of beauty, including each of us—our own talents, our own purposes. We are all very special and talented in our own ways.

The meadows and forests would be quite still if only birds that sang the best were allowed to sing.

RESPONSIBLE AND RESPECTFUL
Are intertwined for success and happiness.

During my childhood, there were many more adults in my life than children. That suited me fine. They all had stories of what they or acquaintances had experienced—past, present, and future hopes and plans. Even my great grandpa, who was the most imaginative and progressive, spoke in simple language children could understand. I imagined being in their stories and experiencing life in their world. Years of living gave them wisdom and understanding beyond a child's scope, beyond a young adult's scope. They were a treasure and worthy of love and respect!

My work experience in Japan during the 90s was one of my most pleasant. Everyone was nice. Everything was completed correctly and on time. Life and work were peaceful and rewarding. It all seemed vaguely familiar as if I had been there before. I hadn't.

My arrival home to Los Angeles and LAX quickly brought me back to the real world. At the baggage claim before customs, I heard an American yelling his disapproval at another. He wasn't responsible, he said, and it was obvious he had no respect for authority. I cringed at the loud disruption and wished I could leave. I felt sorry for the loud distraught man. Did he know any peace? His angry outburst answered, 'No.'

My two months working and living among the Japanese in Osaka revealed two secrets of their success. Principles I experienced in Japan were the same I experienced growing up on the farm—principles within the group mentality of the Japanese culture and the independent Iowa farmer. One has few natural resources and lives in cramped surroundings. The other has bountiful resources and wide-open spaces.

Self-responsibility is the first secret. Japanese adhere to the principle I heard so many times in rural Iowa, "A chain is only as strong as its weakest link." When chores need to be done and you don't do your job, an animal goes hungry or worse. You forget to shut the chicken house door at night and a fox kills the chickens. You reap what you sow, positive and negative.

The second secret is respect. We must respect ourselves before we can respect others. Group mentality cannot be successful without respect. Corporations cannot flourish without respect. A family cannot succeed without respect.

A farmer learns respect as a child. Nature is a powerful and sometimes unfair teacher. Farmers learn to take what nature hands out, being thankful when she is kind and resourceful when she is not. Resilience and self-reliance are common traits of successful farmers and successful Japanese. Neither can afford weak links in their chain toward success.

Self-responsibility and self-reliance work hand-in-hand. When you are self-reliant, you manage your actions. We all know we make our luck, our future, our success. Don't waste energy competing with others and blaming others for your failures. The definition of a loser is not one who fails, but rather one who blames others for their failure. Everyone can see through an excuse.

People may offer you an excuse—which is not kind, just more poison. There are no excuses, only reasons. An excuse is a quick dodge and permanent. Achievement is temporary and hard. Take responsibility for your actions. Work toward your goals and compete only with yourself. You will be amazed by your limitless growth and happiness!

Every choice we make results in a consequence. Choose wisely and always be responsible and respectful.

When was the first time you felt responsible in front of people other than your family? Mine was the day the country school teacher told me I was big enough to get the daily water for the school. An older student would help me. The job was to walk a quarter mile to a neighboring farm and back, carrying the pail of water between us.

The weather did not affect getting water. The day was cold and overcast, with snow in the forecast. Carrying the water back to school was difficult. My hands were cold and my arms were tired, but I loved it. I loved it for the feeling it gave me.

My teacher had given me something more valuable than any amount of book learning I may have missed. She gave me responsibility and demonstrated her faith in me. A wonderful gift to a child!

Whatever happens in your life, it is up to you how you respond to it. There are no excuses. You have complete ownership of your life. Choose to take full responsibility. This philosophy will put you ahead, rising above all those blaming others and circumstances. You can make life happen for you, not to you. Take ownership!

INTEGRITY
Like attitude, encompasses and affects every part of your life.

Honesty, Truth, Integrity are the foundation of a successful and happy life. For any kind of lasting success, it must be real.

Every action has a reaction. Building a life, a career, a business or a relationship on a solid foundation gives assurance and peace of mind. A house of cards may have a wonderful appearance but soon topples. A relationship without truth and honesty is like quicksand pulling you down.

Begin with self-honesty. Are you honest and open about who you are? Honesty and integrity are not situational or relevant to circumstances. Rationalizing, 'others do it, so it's okay for me to do the same' or 'it's not as bad as most' is immature and never builds a reputation of high integrity. Everyone wants to work and be with people we trust. Leaders must be trustworthy. You may not lead millions, but you lead your children and those you wish to help.

We know what is right and wrong at a young age. Do your own litmus test if something is questionable. Is it true? Truth is absolute. Is it ethical? Is it honest? Then you proceed or not. Stand up for truth when you are under pressure. Don't believe, "A little white lie hurts no one." It does. Little white lies lead to bigger white lies. Big white lies lead to lies that ruin lives.

A person's presence speaks genuine and true OR pretentious and fictional.

Am I on a soapbox? Yes, I guess I am. I have experienced and watched what lies have done. I have also experienced genuinely honest people. What a calm relaxing feeling to be with and learn from those in whom you have complete trust.

Everyone who knew my father would agree his word was worth its weight in gold. It never wavered. What he said was the absolute truth. Truthfulness and raising his children were very important to him. He wanted me to enjoy the rewards of truthfulness. How he taught me to be truthful may be frowned on by many, but it worked for me. No, I wasn't traumatized. It helped me have clear and easy-to-follow boundaries, which I wish for all children.

He told me, "If you lie, the old devil will get you." It was not a threat, more like a passing comment. I didn't think the old devil sounded good and where would he take me? I had seen drawings of the devil with horns and a tail. My imagination filled in the details.

One night, I dreamed he was standing very close to my bed and staring at me. He didn't look exactly like the picture. Instead, he was a small, red and black creature with little horns, a tail, and a hideous face. I didn't want to see that ugly little creature again. And who knows what else my imagination would have added.

Am I truthful? Some say, "To a fault." The fault is not in hurting feelings. There is always a positive compliment you can give in place of agreeing the horrible looking dress is beautiful. Losing opportunities by giving credit to others when credit is due and never wavering on integrity when making decisions are not faults. They are the right thing to do. In return, my rewards have been many, including invaluable peace of mind and no regrets.

I thank my father and the ugly little creature in my dream for keeping me on the truthful path.

Choosing honesty, truth and integrity will give an inner winning with victories no one can take from you. All successful relationships are built on mutual trust. Doesn't everyone want truthful friends and colleagues? People who give their honest opinion and advice. Differing opinions, assessed and filtered, are necessary for growth.

Ask yourself three questions when making a decision and before proceeding. Is it necessary? Is it true? Is it kind?

SUPPORTING ACT
A valued perspective for keeping ego in check.

Supporting act is a term normally used in entertainment and where I learned the value of being a supporting act. I offered a fast, colorful act. It was used as the opening act for the Harlem Globetrotters and stage shows. At rodeos, it was used to add variety and family entertainment.

The act I created, perfected, and performed was the product. The product was placed where it best supported the event. I was proud of my product and its popularity. It was authentically me, but the applause was for the product I shared.

Separating yourself from your product is important when dealing with self-worth and ego. A fleeting fling of self-importance is different from being a full-fledged egotist. I have seen inflated egos ruin personal and professional lives.

Don Sartell shares my displeasure of egotism gone amok. He wrote *The Little Book with the Big Ego*. Two of his quotes I particularly like, "Egotism is like a bubble. We all know what happens to a bubble." "Celebrity and big mouths sometimes live together. Pride whispers, ego shouts."

Hopefully, we all are 'star quality' supporting acts, supporting things greater than ourselves. Being a great supporter of family and community has the potential to change the world. It begins with you. You don't have to be a celebrity. Celebrities would not exist in a world populated only by them. In reality, they are supporting acts for events and causes.

Being a leader and a supporting act is not an oxymoron. They both are necessary to possess and be used in our various life roles. Successful parents, teachers, and spouses are leaders as well as supporters.

FULFILLING A NEED
From a vision to building, adapting, leading and supporting to fulfill a need.

You must be present and attentive to know the circumstances, purpose and pathways to the desired outcome. If there is no clear vision, how can you develop a roadmap? What is your Why, your Purpose? How are you going to achieve your goals and fulfill your purpose?

My daughter, Rhonda, grew up in Chicago and spent all her free time with Grandpa on the farm. She saw farming firsthand. She knew the work and planning involved in providing products for food, clothing and shelter.

Her city friends lacked the knowledge to understand the importance of farmers and the farming profession. They saw 'the farm' as cool and a fun adventure. Farmers didn't wear suits and ties. How important could they be?

Rhonda was determined that farmers receive the respect they deserve. We co-founded Thank A Farmer® and drew on our combined strengths to reach our goals. She was the creative arm, designing a fun and informative program for children. I was the marketing and booking arm.

With years of teaching twirling and child-development courses, I knew how smart and flexible children are. Children are curious and open-minded. Teaching children empowers the child and they will teach their family and friends.

Live educational programs were nearly nonexistent at fairs and livestock shows. Could we attract audiences? Without risk there is nothing. We would start small, be patient, lead by example, and exceed expectations in quality and service.

Our Thank A Farmer programming fulfilled a need and quickly became successful. We bought another set of sound and props, I learned the program and did the dates when Rhonda was already booked and unavailable. We crisscrossed the U.S. nonstop. Our courage, conviction and commitment were unlimited.

Every venue varied, so we had to be flexible and adapt. The two things we guarded were preserving the quality of our program and customer comfort. We were firm in what was needed for a classroom-type environment providing value and comfort to our audiences. Regardless of detailed information sent, there were times the presentation area was next to a pen of baby goats or a barn of crowing and clucking chickens or audiences facing the sun.

It is never easy doing something that hasn't been done. But, it is guaranteed to be exciting and challenging! Everyone involved has a learning curve. Collective segments make the whole. The value of each segment determines the value of the whole. The requirement is doing the best you can with what you have where you are.

Thank A Farmer led agricultural organizations to a new style of Ag education and introduced the importance of teaching children. We led and supported. We led our cause and were a supporting segment of the venue, its mission, and agriculture.

What need do you see? Are you willing to constructively build, adapt, lead and support to fulfill the need?

EVERYDAY LEADING
Simply stepping out in front with an objective and sharing what you know.

As a leader, you must conduct yourself in a manner worthy of imitation. What you do speaks louder than your words. And, your words must match what you do. Without the experience of doing, leadership is an empty theory. Leading comes after doing.

In high school I never thought of myself as a leader. I never held an office in any of the organizations. It was enough shock to my system coming from a one-room country school of 12–16 students in the whole school to 40 in one classroom. I preferred teaching what I knew to a few at a time, resulting in teaching up to 100 baton students per week, during high school, with no more than five in a class.

My style of leadership is derived through need, common sense and doing. I teach my expertise and lead by example. Personalities and mindsets of leaders and followers are not in a textbook.

Noticing how the "in clique" of girls ran over the majority, in high school I created the Pomettes. In place of dance and twirl routines, it was dance and pom-poms. We each made two oversized pom-poms, one white and one red, which provided flexibility in creating varied patterns. I was the teacher, as well as a participant, and a stickler on precision and showmanship, not an easy combination.

Even though I was only 16 when we started, I thought of the participants as my girls. My girls made me proud. They worked hard and delivered. We performed at hometown games and even traveled to an away engagement. I loved seeing my girls spotlighted and recognized. And, I learned leading a larger group was as easy as a few.

In the animal world, the leader leads with no thought of how many are following. I will use Old Guernsey, a tall, bony, yellow and white cow, as an example. It is unlikely the herd called her a leader. We did. She was the only milk cow in the herd of stocky beef cattle.

Every spring we moved the herd from fields where they were easily fed during the winter to a pasture of green grass with trees for shade during the summer. They were driven through our farm buildings to the road, up the road, by another farm's buildings and into a lane leading to their summer pasture.

The first move was very difficult, cattle running to every opening they could see. Old Guernsey stayed her course, right in the middle of the road, and took her direction from us. She was calm and focused.

When we moved them back for the winter, she knew the way. Stepping out to the lead, her long legs kept the others hurrying to keep up with no time for distractions. Every year after, she got to the front and made a quick and easy job of moving the cattle. She was the leader.

We thought she was the smartest cow ever. The lead cow never steps in the manure of those in the herd following. And, she has first shot at the freshest grass!

Are you a leader? Or, do you prefer being only as good as what you are following? Challenge yourself to be the best you can be and you will lead. Be an example to imitate. Organizations have a leader, a leader in every department and every team.

You are the leader of your life. Are you inspiring yourself by your work ethic, your achievements, your attitude, your focus, your consistency, your integrity? Do you want your children imitating a person like you? They do, you know.

21st CENTURY LEADERSHIP
Be attentive to change and valued principles

It is 2019 and what you know about leadership may be wrong. Who you lead and how you lead is no longer the 20th-century style of command and control. There are more women working than men.

Millennials are the largest group to enter the workforce. They grew up in an era of abundance and overcompensating parents, not the Happy Days of the 50s or the Corporate 70s.

It is predicted that by 2020 millennials will fill 50% of the leadership positions where there will be five generations in the workforce. Ethnic minorities will be the majority by 2042 and the working majority by 2045. The 21st century is deemed the century for women.

Business journals write what has changed from the 20th century to the 21st century:

- financial capital to human capital

- economical skill to emotional intelligence

- command-and-control dictating structure to collaborative and facilitating.

Twenty-first century leadership is aligning and purpose driven. It is getting people to stand tall, find confidence and think for themselves, developing self-motivated leaders turned loose.

As the leader, any dissatisfaction, uncertainty, and quality issues point to you. You are the problem. The buck stops with the leader.

There are no bad soldiers under a good general."

-Napoleon Bonaparte.

Leaders are under intense scrutiny. Technology records their every move. Plus, media outlets are competing for attention. The leader has to be the best example of everything he/she wants the followers to be:

- a self-manager
- consistent
- honest

Followers will watch and imitate, unconsciously mirror and match. It is the 'connected age.'

Technology has changed and procedures may have changed, but business and people fundamentally haven't changed. People have wanted and still want to be moved, validated, respected, cared for and appreciated.

Each generation is shaped by national events occurring in their lives.

- Wars shaped Baby Boomers in commitment to fulfill duty.

- Gen Xers grew up with MTV, Watergate, O.J., the Challenger disaster. Their predominant goals are to make money and pursue achievement.

- Millennials have trust issues due to the internet boom with its issues and WikiLeaks. They want freedom, flexibility and value in helping others. They want thoughtful feedback, quickly. Leaders learn how to adapt, be versatile and flexible in showing them progress and that what they do matters.

Women outnumber men in the workforce. They bring their innate attributes; connectedness, collaboration, social values and emotional intelligence. Fortune 500 firms with the most female board members outperformed those with the least by 26% on return of invested capital and a 16% return on sales. Women control 85% of all retail. They are under-represented in leadership and partner relations.

Leaders must leverage unique talents of men and women, young and old, be authentic, empathetic and mission driven. Successful leaders point out everyone's uniqueness and how to utilize it, provide opportunities to work together, do mentoring and reverse mentoring. They must be a student learner, ask questions and listen. Be the change they want to see.

My favorite leaders are candid, positive and visionary. Former General Electric boss Jack Welch's leadership style easily spans the 20th and 21st centuries. He says the role of a leader is:

- Chief Meaning Officer: Where? Why going? What's in it for them?

- Chief Broomer: getting rid of clutter

- Generosity gene: no jealousy, loves people's success

- Chief Fun Officer: have fun, celebrate little victories and big victories, create excitement

Success magazine wrote, "Leadership is all about growing others. It's about your team and its welfare. It's about your direct reports and their performance. Leadership is a tough act. It's a daily balancing act. As a leader, you're expected to use your insight, experience and rigor to balance the conflicting demands of short- and long-term results."

So, what do leaders do? Does leadership have rules? Jack Welch says so in his classic 2009 book, *Winning*, which he wrote with Suzy Welch. His 8 Rules of Leadership are as follows.

1. Leaders relentlessly upgrade their team, using every encounter as an opportunity to evaluate, coach and build self-confidence.

2. Leaders make sure people not only see the vision, but they also live and breathe it.

3. Leaders get into everyone's skin, exuding positive energy and optimism.

4. Leaders establish trust with candor, transparency, and credit.

5. Leaders have the courage to make unpopular decisions and gut calls.

6. Leaders probe and push with a curiosity that borders on skepticism, making sure the questions are answered with action.

7. Leaders inspire risk-taking and learning by setting the example.

8. Leaders celebrate, creating an atmosphere of recognition and positive energy.

A quote with no expiration date,

"Before you are a leader, success is all about growing yourself. When you become a leader, success is all about growing others."

-Jack Welch

Growing and strengthening yourself comes before leading and growing others, which is the same advice I received from a Navajo medicine man, Jones Benally. Jones is a man of few words. He is a celebrated hoop dancer and a very wise man.

One afternoon I spoke with Jones about difficult relationships. We agree on philosophy. But he can say in few words what takes me many. "Good to work with others. First must be strong. Like a tree. Stand on own. Not lean on others. They walk away. You fall down."

When the hospital has a difficult case and has used all modern medicines to no avail, they call in their respected staff member, Jones Benally. He sees what he can do with herbs and bodywork. He says, "I am proud of myself to be able to work with my people and help."

Jones is in his 90s and is currently dancing, teaching and helping!

Grow and share your strengths. Your strengths benefit you, your family, colleagues and acquaintances. Be proactive and a valued member of the 21st Century!

Section Three
DO IT!

OVERCOMING FEAR
It is possible!

Some people only talk about what they are going to do. Others talk about what they are going to do, plan, prepare, are all set, and stop in their tracks. They are afraid to do it. Fear doesn't qualify as an excuse or good reason. Be courageous and do it! Nothing happens without action.

> *"What we think or what we know or what we believe is, in the end, of little consequence. The only consequence is what we do."*
> -John Ruskin

We all experience fear in our lives. Sometimes fear comes as little twinges that quickly pass and other times it can be overwhelming. When you are very afraid, really fearful, what are your physical symptoms?

It's my stomach, but never again like at my first baton twirling contest. I had never been involved in any activity outside my country school, my parents were the only people I knew, and I didn't know what I was supposed to do. I was really scared! My stomach started doing contortions as I had never experienced. I knew I was going to vomit if I didn't faint first. I told my father that I was very sick and was going to vomit.

I couldn't believe his lack of sympathy when he said, "If you have to vomit, you'd better get it done because they are getting ready to call your name."

I said, "I'm too sick, I can't twirl."

"Sure, you can. You have to. Go show them what you can do." He smiled and looked so confidently at his terrified daughter. Little did I know the significance of my father's foresight and strength at that moment. It was the beginning of a role he played in my life.

He was a quiet and shy man, but when he said, "You can do it," you could. In high school, he set track records that held for over 30 years. He once said, "I ran so fast at the state meet because I'd never been to Iowa City and was so scared—I ran as fast as I could to find the end." He understood my fright and was determined to help me beat it.

As for fear—when what you fear has no bearing on your safety, do not let it control you. Thanks to my father not allowing fear to stop me, I did my twirls and was awarded second place at that little contest with five contestants. That second-place trophy is one of my most cherished. It symbolizes the day fear did not win. The day I learned fear is only a reaction, an emotional response to perceived danger.

Courage is a decision. Have courage and face fear head-on. Claim victory! As Ralph Waldo Emerson simply said,

"Do the thing you fear, and the death of fear is certain."

If your dream or what you desire is greater than your fear, you will have the courage to squelch the fear and be on your way.

Fear is one of the greatest obstacles to success and happiness. Our mindset determines if fear wins over us or dies. It comes from our minds, our ego, our imagination. Fear is what we think or imagine might happen—not what *will* happen.

Psychologists like to use the acronym, *Fantasized Experiences Appearing Real.* Since the prime source of our fears comes from us, we have power over them. If you would like my proven fear antidote, read on. It works!

Fear cannot exist in the present when you intently focus on the task at hand, the present task and next step. Your focus on the task at hand leaves no room for fear-laden mind-talk.

As a child, I was afraid to shut up the chickens when it was dark. The noises of little nocturnal creatures and the corn rustling in the breeze made me shiver in fear. I imagined werewolves stalking and preparing to pounce. Out of desperation came a cure. Whistling blocked out other noises. I whistled a happy tune all the way to and from the chicken house. It worked. Concentrating on whistling and doing my job didn't leave room for werewolf fears.

I used a similar concept years later when performing a solo presentation: in competition, in the middle of a stadium or basketball court, on stage, featured on national television or keynoting to aerospace corporations. It is a simple fear antidote that never fails me and won't fail you.

There are only two steps, two very important steps that must have your full commitment.

- Step # 1: Visualize a positive outcome, repeating over and over preceding the event and as you approach the performance area.

- Step # 2: During the presentation, focus only on the task at hand and what comes next. Your mind will be busy, with no room left for fear.

A bonus: Once you are confident fear is 'left in the dust,' look your audience in their eyes and telegraph, 'I love you and am here for you.' Audiences feel your true emotions. Prepare yourself beforehand, then forget about yourself. Focus on your task and audience.

Acting in spite of fear is called courage. Be courageous. Visualize a positive outcome, focus on the task at hand, do what you fear. You are now courageous, claiming victory over fear!

As for the ever-popular Fear of Failure, I have a question. How can you win without first failing? Winning is what we all strive for, but we don't learn much when winning; at least I never did. It was failing when I learned and came back stronger and better.

Failure is a win in learning. View failure as a learning opportunity. When you fail, you have the opportunity to learn what didn't work and devise a new plan for the next try. The faster you fail and try again, the faster you move forward in achieving your goal.

Thomas Edison, the world record patent holder, embraced each failure as a step on the road to success. He said,

Think it! Work it! Do it!

"I didn't fail. I just found 10,000 ways that didn't work."

Be like Edison . . . believe, persist, achieve . . . in that order.

PROBLEM TO ADVANTAGE
Accept the gift and build on it.

A problem doesn't need to stop you. Work around it. It may become your advantage.

While serving in the navy, Humphrey Bogart received facial injuries causing a lisp. He feared the lisp would keep him out of movies. Instead, it became an asset, perfect for his tough guy roles.

I love this centuries-old quote. An Athenian who was lame in one foot was laughed at by the other soldiers on account of his lameness. He said,

> *"I am here to fight. Not to run."*

That attitude makes for success in all aspects of life, any place and any time in the world.

My problem in twirling was finding a teacher who could teach beyond the basics. I attended a twirling camp for a week each summer to learn new twirls, go home and practice all year. When I developed a problem I couldn't overcome, I would ask my father to help me. He would ask, "Where does it start and where is it supposed to end?"

He taught me how to apply the principles of physics. Understanding the physics of twirling opened doors of creativity and innovation. It enabled me to create material complementing each individual student's style and ability, setting them apart.

Einstein was right,

"In the middle of difficulty lies opportunity."

A problem gets your attention and you rise to meet the challenge. It is a stimulus for creativity, innovation and change. Oliver Wendell Holmes said,

"Man's mind once stretched by a new idea never regains its original dimensions."

Every problem you solve adds to your knowledge, confidence, independence, security and freedom.

HABITS
Enemies or allies?

WHO AM I?

I am your constant companion.
I am your greatest asset or heaviest burden.
I will push you up to success or down to disappointment.
I am at your command.
Half the things you do might just as well be turned over to me,
For I can do them quickly, correctly and profitably.
I am easily managed, just be firm with me.
Those who are great, I have made great.
Those who are failures, I have made failures.
I am not a machine, though I work with the precision of a
Machine and the intelligence of a person.
You can run me for profit, or you can run me for ruin.
Show me how you want it done. Educate me. Train me.
Lead me. Reward me.
And I will then ... do it automatically.
I am your servant.
Who am I?
I am a habit.

-Author unknown

Have you noticed that forming a good habit is harder than forming a bad habit? And breaking a good habit is easier to break than a bad habit?

Knowledge is valuable, but knowing something is very different from making it an important part of reaching your goals. Knowledge has to be activated, like wood for a bonfire. The wood may be very dry or doused with gasoline, set for combustion, but until a spark ignites it, it just sits there.

You must provide the spark to set your knowledge into action. Once you know what is needed to achieve your goal, do it *every day* and it will become a habit. Repetition, repetition, repetition develops habits. Since habits are formed by repetition, beware of repeating detrimental actions. We choose what we want to develop as a habit.

With set habits, we don't have to think. We just run the program. Experts say it can take three to twelve months to get a habit fully ingrained, depending on the individual. For me, a habit that I know is important to my success takes a week. How long does it take you?

Time restraints vary from day to day. When I miss a day, I get back on track. Do not break good habits. I have found my easiest and surest way to achievement is through the force of habit. I believe the same for you.

There are many systems and programs to motivate and instill timelines to achievement. I prefer simplicity and ease. Simply determine what needs to be done daily to improve and make it a habit. You won't dread it or even think about it. It is programmed into your subconscious. You automatically do it. Ninety-five percent of thinking is an unconscious habitual process.

The years I was preparing for the National Championship competition, my habit was practicing my two-minute and thirty-second competition routine 10 times every day. My practice was very focused and intense. Each routine was timed with the number of breaks and drops noted. I developed habits within habits. Every day I tried to beat all the previous day's evaluations. The competition was within myself which, I believe is the surest path to success.

Keeping an accurate daily evaluation system was valuable for me and will be for you, your team and organization. What was accomplished? What was working and what was not? What needs to be eliminated or added? What needs improvement and how can it be done? Set an evaluation system to fit your improvement needs.

There are times when nothing seems to work properly, testing your commitment and persistence. There are also plateaus, working and showing no improvement. Plateaus happen. Be patient. You may need to assess and adjust, OR think of a plateau as coasting time before the uphill climb to improvement. Be tolerant, but never lose your drive to improve every day and reach your goals.

A mountain-climbing expedition was attempting to climb Mt McKinley when they encountered a blinding storm. They camped for the night and decided to go down. When they returned, they found their camp only 18 feet from the top. Too often we give up when only a little more effort or patience is needed to reach the top.

Make persistent and patient habits and reach your goals. Track your progress with consistency. Attention to improvement is rewarding and fun.

TOTAL FITNESS
Mandatory for excellent health and for elevating success.

We take care of our homes, cleaning, repairing, upgrading. We clean and service our cars, making sure the tires are good and it has gas to keep running. What about our bodies?

If we had to pay ten million dollars for our bodies, we'd take better care of them. They are our housing and a vehicle rolled into one with hundreds of parts and thousands of functions, a true miracle.

Unlike houses and cars, our bodies are living cells needing rest to rejuvenate, replenish and stay healthy. Are you allowing enough time for rest, or are you cheating and paying the consequences?

What about the fuel you are putting in your body? Is it sustaining or a quick fix, short-lived and damaging?

Are you physically active or are you allowing sludge and rust to build up? Our bodies were made to be active. With modern conveniences lessening physical exertion, we must consciously exercise.

I-Min Lee, professor of medicine at Harvard Medical school spoke at Iowa State U. in 2016. The title of her talk was "Physical Activity: Wonder Drug for Chronic Disease Prevention."

In a 2012 paper published in the journal *Lancet*, Lee and her colleagues established that reducing the rate of physical inactivity by 25% could prevent more than one to three million deaths worldwide every year. They estimated that physical inactivity causes six percent of the burden of disease from coronary heart disease, seven percent of type 2 diabetes, 10% of breast cancer and 10% of colon cancer. "The risk of premature death from a sedentary lifestyle is similar to that of smoking," Lee said in an interview with BBC.

My attitude and my energy levels are directly tied to exercise. I can be doing everything else right, but without regular exercise, I can feel my attitude heading downward.

I have a friend who is 70 and looks 60. When I saw her the other day I said, "Sally, you are looking great."

She said "I feel great. I got a second job."

"A second job? But I thought your gift shop was flourishing."

"It is, but my second job is 30 minutes on the treadmill every day at 7:00 am. You know you have to show up for jobs. Now it's a habit. Not good in dollars, but great in health and attitude benefits."

Exercise is the #1 "stress buster." And, don't fool yourself, stress is a killer. In fact, the World Health Organization estimates that 80% of all illnesses are directly or indirectly caused by stress. Therefore, if you're not proactive in busting stress, it's very likely to come back and bust you!

I've been fortunate to have physically challenging work throughout my life. Work where strength and energy are necessary. Baton twirling is a full-body exercise requiring balance, flexibility, body and eye-hand coordination, stamina, neural pathways for coordinating quick and fluid mind/body messaging. And this is why I still practice some form of twirling nearly every day.

I learned in world competition, a fraction makes the difference. Being in peak physical condition was a necessity, which meant training, eating the right food, getting plenty of rest. I did all required and still needed more oxygen and more energy. If I hadn't trained, I wouldn't have been able to use my personal resources to the fullest.

Using our personal resources to the fullest requires more than physical fitness. It requires total fitness:

- Physical
- Mental
- Emotional
- Spiritual
- Social

To be most effective, happiest and to live life with purpose, we must be totally fit.

A tall order, right? Plus, we are bombarded with conflicting information from the media and acquaintances. "Eat this." "No, not that." "This exercise." "No, this is the best." "Coffee is good for you." "Coffee is bad for you."

Nearly all guidelines change with time and with various experts. Since we are unique individuals, our needs are also unique. There is no one-size-fits-all. What works for someone else may not work for you.

Pay attention to what your body tells you. Listen! It will tell you what foods give you sustained energy and what foods drag you down. What type of exercise, and how much, gives you energy and strength? How much sleep do you need to feel rested and at your best?

You are the only one who knows. Doctors and advisors hear only what you tell them. When you seek advice, seek it from a knowledgeable and excellent role model. Test the advice. How does it make you feel? Too often, we don't listen to our bodies and blindly follow the one-size-fits-all concept.

Unless we have been living under a rock, we all know how exercise combats stress and strengthens the heart. What about the lymphatic system? We all have one, and I believe it is one of the most important systems. It starts in our fingers and toes, goes up through our lymph nodes and empties out into our thoracic area.

The reason the lymphatic system is so important, it pulls excess protein, bacteria, garbage, and toxins out of our system to keep it purified. Lymphatic experts say, "If the lymphatic system is working properly, it is nearly impossible to get sick. It is the first line of defense against disease."

The problem is, it doesn't have a pump to pump it through the body. The heart pumps the blood. There is three times more lymph than blood and no pump. Lymph is moved by muscle contraction. It is forced through one-way valves. Unless we are moving the lymph just sits, builds up toxins and poisons, and we are more susceptible to disease.

Take a look at this media headline and article:

ISU WILL LEAD NEW NATIONAL "SUPERBUG" INSTITUTE

Dan Grooms has been appointed the next Dean of the College of Veterinary Medicine at Iowa State University. He will begin Oct. 1, 2018. Grooms, an expert in bovine infectious diseases, earned a bachelor's degree in animal science from Cornell University and two degrees from Ohio State University—a veterinary medicine degree and a Ph.D. in veterinary preventive medicine, with a specialty in veterinary virology.

Why is this significant?

The Association of Public and Land-grant Universities (APLU) and the Association of American Veterinary Medical College (AAVMC) have tabbed Iowa State to lead a new national institute focused on addressing a global public health concern: antimicrobial resistance. The creation of the Institute for Antimicrobial Resistance Research and Education was announced July 26 in response to a 2015 APLU/AAVMC report that identified antimicrobial resistance as a top global health and environmental issue.

The institute will be led by Paul Plummer (Ph.D. 2009 vet microbiology), ISU associate professor of veterinary diagnostic and production animal medicine, with leadership also coming from the University of Nebraska, the University of Iowa, and the Mayo Clinic.

Each year in the U.S., at least two million people become infected with bacteria resistant to antibiotics, and 23,000 people die as a direct result of these infections. Many more die from other conditions complicated by an antibiotic-resistant infection, according to the Centers for Disease

Control and Prevention. These drug-resistant "superbugs" also harm the ecosystem and cost multi-billions annually in medical costs and economic losses.

"Antimicrobial resistance touches each of us in our daily lives," Plummer says. "This new institute provides a great resource for the entire country as we work to build strong, collaborative research and educational programs to mitigate this risk."

A strong immune system will be vital as more superbugs develop. We must actively do our part in keeping healthy and not having to rely on the 'magic pill or shot.' Exercise, rest and eat nutritious food. Allow your miracle body to protect itself and function at its top-level.

As we age, we find some things are easy and others aren't so easy anymore. My friend jokingly says, "Rolling out of bed in the morning is easy. Getting off the floor is a whole other story."

Your health is your wealth. With good health, it is possible for you to create wealth, but your wealth cannot buy good health. Wealth can help repair minimal problems, but grave problems are manifested over time.

To elevate your performance level in all areas of your life, you must take care of your body. Exercise. Eat whole foods, those found around the periphery of a grocery store. Food in boxes with a prolonged shelf life may last forever but will steal years from your life and productivity. What you eat affects your mood, energy, attitude . . . your performance level.

During my competitive years, many competitors ate chocolate bars before competing. It gave them an extra boost of energy. I tried it. Once! It gave me weakness and confusion. No more chocolate before competition or half-time performances.

Ten years later my joints were painful and weak. I experienced brief periods when all I could see was white as if a white sheet had dropped in front of my eyes. The 'white-outs' signaled time to see a doctor. The pies, cakes, cinnamon rolls I loved to bake and eat were triggering hypoglycemia to the point of white-outs and acute inflammation of joints. Like sugar, stimulants plummeted my blood sugar levels. Eliminating sugar and stimulants was the only answer to revive my health.

No coffee, no cinnamon rolls? It is a small price to pay for feeling energized and healthy. I learned to use food cautiously and as a fuel, not for pleasure. If we all want to perform like a world-class athlete, we must choose the best fuel for our body.

Society is visually judgmental. Are you pleased by how your body represents your brand, character and emotional maturity? If not, you can change your eating and exercising habits.

You control your health and success. Eliminate temptations and replace them with healthy substitutes. Simplicity and convenience will help you keep on track. Your increased performance level will be motivating.

It is your responsibility to nurture and maintain your health. Keep prevention forefront. Listen to your body. Learn to hear a slight discord. Correct it before it becomes a sour note that ends up destroying the beautiful song—the song of life. Your body will tell you what is good and bad for it. Pay attention, be responsible and relish the rewards of good health.

COMPETITION

No one is exempt.
Competition stokes the fire within.

Like it or not, you are in competition. Securing 'your place in the sun' or a place in line at the supermarket, you are competing. Other people want your place. Getting what you want and the quality you want is your responsibility. The higher the stakes, the more effort is needed.

You must know your competition. How much do you need to improve to be a contender and eventually be #1? Seeing world-class performers at the beginning of my baton career was a valuable gift. I saw what was possible. It gave me a clear understanding of my position and what was needed to be a competitor.

My dream of being the world's best was no longer in a dream state. It was in the real world, the real world of competition for a coveted position. Now what? I decided I would work twice as hard as all the great twirlers and catch up to them.

Work to improve what you know. Outstanding accomplishment brings outstanding help and possibilities. Be alert and attentive to all possibilities.

In high school, I practiced in the gym, on the stage, in the halls, any place there was room. On the farm I practiced anyplace there was a level hard spot. There was no cement, so the dirt would soon become a dust bowl, the grass was uneven, the road had loose gravel but that didn't matter. My theory was if I can do it when the conditions are tough, won't it be easy with good conditions? I even practiced facing the sun.

In the process, I broke my nose three times, acquired weekly major bruises such as a black eye and cut lips. But the result, torn up turf on a football field, spotlights in my eyes and, of course, the sun didn't bother me. I had built my flexibility and adaptability. I had learned how to compensate.

You will find that adversity along the way makes it all easier in the end. The old Greek proverb is true,

"A smooth sea never made a skillful mariner."

I twirled batons at almost every function in Iowa, even on top of a drive-in movie concession stand. It had a large flat roof. It wasn't unusual to see entertainment there at intermission, just not a baton twirler! I was so eager to excel that I would take every opportunity for experience. Whatever it is you want to accomplish, seize every opportunity to improve and perfect it.

Nothing is more motivating than upcoming competition. Keep in mind, preparation determines the outcome! If your commitment and energy need to be invigorated, visualize your competition. Then, visualize you are a step above the competition. Feel it. Enjoy it.

Many years ago, a movie studio was casting a new western called *The Lone Ranger*. The casting call was for the leading man. Many actors were auditioning, leaving their publicity photos, resumes and hoping for a callback.

Suddenly the door swung open! In the doorway stood a man immaculately dressed in western wardrobe, white hat and black mask. "I am the Lone Ranger!"

The man was Clayton Moore. He was the Lone Ranger from that time on. His preparation and commitment gave him the supreme confidence to walk into that audition as if he already had the job. Preparation and commitment will produce the confidence needed for success in all aspects of life.

Assess your competition, but never waste energy competing against competitors. You have no control over them. You do have control over yourself. Set small goals out of reach. Once you reach them, reset, reach, reset, reach until you have reached your desired pinnacle.

During the 2002 Winter Olympics, Michelle Kwan was the most decorated skater in U.S. history. The four-time world champion women's skater was hands down predetermined to win it all. She had extensive media coverage and endorsements.

Before the Olympics, feeling overly confident she had the win, she terminated her long-time coach and her choreographer. When the *Today Show* asked her, "Why?" she replied, "I want the world to know that I can win on my own without the help from coaches."

During the most important competition of her life, to win the Olympic Gold medal, Michelle two-footed her triple toe loop and fell. She finished third behind rival Irina Slutskaya of Russia and U.S. skater Sarah Hughes, who took first.

Her teammate, 16-year-old Sarah Hughes, listened intently, taking in all her coach had to say. She skated the best skate of her life, doing two flawless quadruple jumps and captured the Gold.

An age-old Proverb warns,

> *"Where there is no counsel, the people fall,*
> *but in counselors there is safety."*

Thinking that we know it all and not questioning our ability, appears before a fall. Success is the biggest threat to success. We become complacent, thinking we know it all.

Learn the new set of skills needed for the new goal. Force a constant mind-learning concept—root out overconfidence. If done, you will not suffer the consequences written in Proverbs 16:18,

> *"Pride goes before destruction*
> *and a haughty spirit before a fall."*

My father was pleased when I won, and that I remembered what he had told me, "There is always someone better." Be grateful for achievements but never over-confident and arrogant.

REINVENTING AND FULFILLING EVER-EXPANDING NEEDS
Capitalize on your knowledge, aptitudes, and strengths.

Have the will to try, faith to believe you can make a difference, and act! You will discover how one success leads to many others. Assess, adjust, adapt and implement as many times as needed.

My daughter and I were performing a comedy variety act at venues from Japan to Madison Square Garden. We adjusted and adapted our shows for all ages; for family, children, corporate break-out sessions to 90-minute concerts. We used the same talent skills for all groups. The difference was presentation style and verbiage.

When 9/11 happened, foreign travel and most corporate work were shut down. I began booking us on free stages at county and state fairs. Many of the smaller fairs did not have adequately sized stages, so we added a magic trick that filled time and required little space. Since they were all agricultural fairs, we decided on 'thank a farmer' for the magic words. The first fair we did the magic trick at was in the middle of dairy country at the Central Wisconsin State Fair.

For the magic to work, we asked the audience to yell the magic words, "Thank a farmer" on the count of three. When they yelled the magic words, we saw several men throughout the audience sit straighter and taller. After the show, one of the dairy farmers came to us and said, "No one has ever thanked me before." Several wives came with tears in their eyes, saying the same and thanking us.

Teenagers came to us with stories about city kids moving into the area, due to development. They were making fun of the farm kids for helping their parents with milking before going to school. After several groups told the same story and seeing the hurt on their faces, my daughter turned to me and said, "They just don't know. We have to teach them."

We developed an entertaining education program teaching the importance of farmers and the contributions of agriculture for a healthy population and economy. Why are farmers important? They grow crops and raise farm animals, generating raw materials for food, clothing and building materials—materials needed for our survival. Farmers deserve to be highly regarded and respected.

Enlightening the minds of millions quickly is impossible. It takes years. Teaching children will be our shortcut. We will teach children. We will empower children with knowledge and respect for farmers. They will teach their families.

Teaching children bite-sized, fun agriculture facts was a new concept for the agricultural industry. For years, they taught information using the concept 'from pasture to plate,' what the farmer grows ends up on your plate. We reversed the direction, using 'plate to pasture,' tracing what the child uses every day back to where it came from. The 'plate to pasture' concept is relatable and personal.

Agricultural organizations believed children needed to be fourth-graders or older to absorb and retain their information. We believe mindset respecting farmers begins in preschool. A positive mindset enhances desire and interest in education.

We dressed in what small children think farmers wear, bib overalls, and built a fun program loaded with fun farm facts. We did simple magic tricks relating to the commodity giving us more time to talk about the visual commodity and use the magic words, 'Thank a farmer.'

The show was interactive containing many questions. We praised those knowing correct answers and thanked all for participating. We used a variety of phrases throughout the program to encourage them to learn and teach others, such as "Your friends won't know this. You can teach them." "Teach your teacher and receive an 'A' for the day." "Grandpa won't know this. You can teach him." They became our little empowered helpers.

My daughter wrote and designed colorful booklets titled, *Fun Farm Facts to Fool Your Family, Friends and Other Fine Folks*. We spoke in words city children could understand the meaning; no agricultural terminology such as acres and bushels. I did the booking and each of us did multiple presentations per day for multiple days at fairs and livestock shows from coast-to-coast and border-to-border.

Our original target age was 5–10-year-old children. We were surprised to see 2-year-old children attentive and participating. Excluding school tour groups, our audiences were equally divided between adults and children. Fun interactive education is fun for all ages.

We worked 11 years at breakneck speed. Did we educate everyone on the importance of farmers and agriculture? Of course not! However, agricultural organizations and commodities began imitating us. They saw the value and success of teaching young children, and teaching children in a language understandable to them. We enthusiastically applaud! They have the funds and resources to educate millions. We hope they keep on track, forever improving and growing every year.

Why is it essential children learn the importance of farmers and the contributions of agriculture for a healthy population and economy? Young children are information sponges and eager to learn and share knowledge with extended families. They are our future teachers and leaders.

When we began Thank A Farmer in 2006, no one was thanking farmers or any other profession. In the last few years, how many local and national campaigns have you seen thanking a profession? I smile when I see numerous professions being thanked, especially "Thank America's Teachers," initiated by Farmers Insurance. By fulfilling a need, we started a movement!

Do you see a need? A need for improving your life or the lives of others? Envision it. What is needed to achieve it? Clarify, strategize and go after it with strong belief, commitment and consistency! When completed, you will experience joyous feelings of satisfaction and accomplishment. Fulfilling needs is a wonderful habit!

CREATE
Be grateful for creativity and protective.

Everyone quotes William Shakespeare, but who did Shakespeare quote? No one. Don't be afraid to be yourself and express yourself—let your uniqueness show. Your uniqueness will no doubt be your catapult to success. There is only one you. And, you have more to contribute than you can imagine. God is not as interested in your ability or inability as He is in your availability!

Martha Graham, the great dancer and choreographer, believed in the uncapped creativity inside each of us.

> *"There is a vitality, a life force, an energy, a quickening that is translated through you into action; and because there is only one of you in all time, this expression is unique. If you block it, it will never exist through another medium and it will be lost. The world will not have it. You must keep that channel open. It is not for*

you to determine how good it is, nor how valuable. Nor how it compares with other expressions. It is for you to keep it yours, clearly and directly."

Diane von Furstenberg, fashion designer, learned through experience to keep her designs hers, clearly and directly. In her words, "At 29, I made the cover of *Newsweek*: I had turned the wrap dress into the fashion hit of the 70s. It was a simple idea, but I felt it was perfect for every woman—from secretaries to celebrities.

We made 25,000 dresses a week, but my business grew so fast that I lost control of it. My design was named after me, Diane von Furstenberg, but the name had lost its meaning once I had licensed the manufacturing rights to just about anyone willing to pay for the privilege.

Within 10 years, I went from designing the hottest dresses around to not being able to convince anyone to carry my merchandise. Everything had disintegrated. I was ashamed.

In 1987, I decided to regain control of my name, my brand. People told me that comebacks in the fashion industry were impossible. I ignored them. It took me 10 years and all my money to start over again.

A long time ago, I decided that my most important dialogues don't take place with other people, they take place with me. I have a real friendship with myself. I am my most ardent critic, my best friend. I am always brutally honest with myself. I always trust myself. So when it came to relaunching my brand, I did what I felt was right."

In 1997, nearly 20 years after disappearing from the fashion industry, Diane von Furstenberg reintroduced her wrap dress. It flew off the racks onto thousands of women.

Protection is not ironclad, but we all must protect our intellectual property using an appropriate copyright, trademark, patent, etc. Intellectual property (IP) refers to creations of the mind, such as inventions; literary and artistic works; designs; and symbols, names and images used in commerce.

Monitoring and protecting intellectual property is time consuming and costly, but very inexpensive compared to starting over. Diane von Furstenberg learned how excessive licensing made her property meaningless.

We created Thank A Farmer and immediately applied for a Thank A Farmer trademark. We received registration. Organizations wanted to buy our thankafarmer.com. Many copied our name and brand. Policing was a full-time job. Attorneys were costly and only used when our trademark attorney needed to remind the perpetrator's attorney of trademark law.

Monsanto was planning a Thank A Farmer national campaign. No attorney would challenge them for less than $1-2M. I was willing and did.

Monsanto had two phone numbers on their website. One was customer service, and the other was media. Customer service kept calling numbers connected to answering machines.

I called the media number and connected with a live person. I said who I was and why I was calling, about trademark infringement. She said the trademark division would call me back. They did in less than an hour.

I had a 30-minute conversation with their top trademark attorney. We were amicable, no blaming or threatening, just truthful. The result was wonderful. They halted all plans for their national Thank A Farmer campaign and kept their word.

During the conversation I said, "I don't understand how Thank A Farmer would work for Monsanto. You sell to all farmers. Wouldn't 'Thank America's Farmers' be more inclusive?" I smiled when I saw Monsanto semis pulling trailers across the country with 'Thank America's Farmers' on the sides.

Protect what is important to you! Be willing to stand against perpetrators. It may not be easy, but know truth wins.

COMMUNICATION
Clear, open and kind.

If you are the only person alive on planet earth, communication is no big deal. Add just one additional person and communication becomes a big deal.

Thinking through the questions *Who? What? Why? When? Where?* and *How?* may seem like overkill to communicate. Yes, it might be when communicating with family or friends because we have programmed those questions into our subconscious. If you are speaking to an audience of 20,000 or communicating as a leader of your team or organization, answer all six questions.

Let's begin with *Who. Who* are you? Are you confident or constantly seeking validation? Do you have a strong sense of self-worth? Self-worth comes from within and with preparation builds confidence. Being authentic, honest and transparent breeds trust and openness. There is never a time for pretense.

Who are they? Have you been curious and asked questions? Have you listened and heard? Have you treated them with respect?

I didn't know Marques Haynes. I had heard the Globetrotters speak of him and always with extreme respect. In fact, they all called him Mr. Haynes in a warm and respectful tone. He had been their star dribbler and captain before retiring. News quickly spread, "Mr. Haynes is coming to the game tonight." I was expecting to see an elderly man, maybe sitting behind the player's bench.

When I finished performing the opening act, I saw a man coming straight toward me, erect posture, quick stride and a big smile. He looked like a *GQ* model and dressed for the most important business meeting of his life. He introduced himself as Marques Haynes. Now I knew why Mr. Haynes was revered. Not only was he immaculately dressed, he spoke as if I was the important person he came to see.

We had a brief conversation, but it took only a few seconds to understand why all the players called him Mr. Haynes. He was generous with his sincere praise given to others. His focused attention gave the recipients value. Marques Haynes had been one of the basketball greats and unrivaled greatest basketball dribbler of all time. He was admired for his ability and was respected for his humble and giving attitude.

What is the topic and focus of communication? The more you know about the topic, the more helpful you can be. If you haven't experienced doing the *What,* tell them. Never ever fake it! A faker is easily spotted and never given a chance for a second impression. People gravitate to and respond to an honest person because they trust them.

Executives hired Rice & Renee to perform at Harmony Land in Japan. Their management had selected a performance stage. It was elevated, in the round with a continuous fountain in a moat-like arrangement between us and the audience. There was no electricity for our sound and equipment. The fountain was noisy and the stage positioning was all wrong. It would make a beautiful picture postcard but could not have been worse for communication with our audiences.

The managers were very proud of their beautiful stage and ready to show us our dressing room. I was thinking, Whoa, this must be changed! With our language barrier, it will be impossible for them to understand how their beautiful staging area can't work. I will have to try.

I looked them in their eyes, each manager, and in a sincere tone slowly said "The stage is beautiful. You pay us a lot of money. We want you to get your money's worth." They smiled and nodded in agreement. "For you to get your money's worth, we need electricity and audience closer. Audience will be very happy. You, very happy too."

The managers got in a huddle and decided on an alternative stage. The engagement was a huge success. When you know *What*, you must speak up so it is a win-win for everyone involved. Kindness and body language can say more than words.

Why? The *Why* is of major importance. It is the most emotional and gets to the root, the purpose. For teams and organizations, have a visual screen and include as many *Why* responses as possible, then narrow down to the clear and strong *Why*. It is also important to know the *Why* of your client. What is their mission? What is their purpose? How are you of benefit to them? Knowing their *Why* enables you to benefit them more than they initially expected.

Where and *When* are logistical and very important in achieving the objective. We've been drilled with, 'Location is everything!' It may not be everything, but who wants to try communicating in a loud and chaotic environment? Too early and premature or too late and passé gives meaning to 'Timing is everything!'

Change and challenges can uproot the best plans. Proactive may turn into adjust, adapt and apply—thinking and communicating on the run. The following demonstrates being proactive, accepting and thriving with change and challenges.

I had flown from Chicago to Los Angeles to appear on the popular Mike Douglas television show. Two months earlier I had made the same trip, but when I arrived, the co-host, Larry Wilcox of *Chips* television fame, refused to work with me. He used up his 'star capital' because he didn't have enough confidence to be vulnerable. He lacked the experience and confidence to understand how controlled vulnerability is the pinnacle of successful communication with an audience.

The show directors were embarrassed and told me, "We'll have you back. Next time you'll be working with a pro." So, here I was again. They wanted to see my routine segments and select what they wanted. That was fine with me. They picked hoop baton, rope spinning and whip cracking plus a separate spot for the whip participation segment.

Dom DeLuise was co-hosting and would happily be my participant. My *When* and *Who* had been changed. It was a blessing. Dom was such a professional. His focus was in making the guest look good, which in turn made him look super. All the while Mike Douglas watched with complete confidence, allowing everyone to do what they did best.

The executive director and producer, Woody Fraser, was delighted. He recommended me and used me for all his shows and pilots wanting a proactive guest with fun audience participation. That one show led to being featured on numerous television shows. I was fortunate to be at the right place at the right time.

How must be done with respect and inclusion. Communication is a two-way street. All you can control is how you communicate and your responses. Are you kind and treat others as they want to be treated? Do you listen intently? Is your voice positive and energized? What is the tone of your voice? Do your eyes dart or do you look in people's eyes? Does your posture denote confidence? Do you keep an open body position toward them? Have you made an effort to look your best? Not in vanity, but in respect to them, which telegraphs their importance to you.

Marques Haynes and Mike Douglas communicated confidence, caring and trust in others. When I think of true gentlemen, I think of Marques Haynes and Mike Douglas and remember how they made me feel. I saw written on a theater's dressing room wall,

> *"People will forget what you said, people will forget what you did, but people will never forget how you made them feel."*

The quote is attributed to Maya Angelou and is essential for all communicators to understand. We must hear and communicate what isn't audible. Dr. Albert Mehrabian, author of *Silent Messages*, conducted several studies on nonverbal communication. He developed a communication model demonstrating that only seven percent of what we communicate consists of the literal content of the message. The use of one's voice, such as tone, intonation and volume, take up 38% and as much as 55% of communication consists of body language.

Peter Drucker once said,

> *"The most important thing in communication is to hear what isn't being said."*

Drucker, described as "the father of modern management" is one of the best-known and most widely influential thinkers and writers on the subject of management theory and practice.

Test this out. First scenario. Go to the grocery store. You are in a hurry. Your eyes are straight ahead and you quickly go in the store and grab a gallon of milk. You rush to the checkout clerk, set the milk on the counter and get payment out as the clerk is ringing up the cost. You pay and leave. Job done. How do you feel? I would guess you are uptight and are thinking, 'Okay, what's next? How quickly can I get it done?'

Second scenario. Go to the grocery store. You are in a hurry. A stranger walks toward you on the way to the milk. Your eyes meet the stranger's eyes and you smile. Smile returned, and no time wasted. You get the milk. On the way to pay, you make eye contact with the boy restocking a shelf. You say, "Good job," and smile as you hurry by. The surprised boy smiles back. No time wasted. When you check out you make eye contact with the clerk and pay. "Have a good day!" is exchanged. You leave, no time wasted. You got the job done and ready for the next. The difference from the first scenario: you are calm, happy and thinking nice people are everywhere.

Go first! Go first with recognizing others with eye contact, a smile, praise or empathy in passing, whatever is appropriate. It won't take any extra time but the rewards are great. Some people refuse to make eye contact. For the ones that do, it may be a wonderful boost for them. I promise it will be for you. What you give away comes back tenfold!

I learned the value of a smile through desperation. You've already read how painfully shy I was and still am at my core. When I was a child, and a stranger asked me a question, I'd smile and nod my head 'Yes' or 'No.' They would always smile back and be satisfied with my answer.

Realizing that when I smiled it calmed my anxiety, and I was braver, I smiled a lot! Smiling at judges in baton competition may have them looking at my smile and missing mistakes I made. Or, they'd like me and not be as harsh in their judging. Same thinking when I did shows. I smiled at all I met on campus at Iowa State. It certainly wasn't my beauty that won all the beauty contests.

Hopefully, I have made the point—

Positive Attracts Positive! Go first!

We have discussed how communication is more than talking. However, talking can be very effective in resolving issues quickly. How you talk with others may be the key. Are you candid with straightforward talk with no third party information and no hidden agendas? Do you bring hard feelings and misunderstandings into the open and don't allow them to fester and grow? Between individuals, keep communication private. Be inclusive with a team. Open communication builds trust which increases ownership and participation.

EXCELLENCE
Strive for excellence and value.

It is a joy to witness excellence.

Constant improvement to achieve excellence is my ever-challenging goal. Mr. Reynolds, our school custodian, opened my eyes to excellence. It is not what you do. It is how well you do it. Quality rises to the top. Rather than focusing only on success, focus on becoming a person of value. When you are of value to others, success and recognition come effortlessly.

> *"You must have, as a basic principle, the determination to achieve excellence in your various fields of endeavor. All labor that uplifts humanity has dignity and importance and should be undertaken with painstaking excellence."*
>
> -Martin Luther King, Jr.

Mr. Reynolds was white-haired and slightly stooped. His office was off the gym, down the stairs to the boiler room in the basement of our school. His overalls were as clean as he kept the school. I saw him when practicing in the gym after other students had gone home. It was also when Mr. Reynolds could get the most done. He kept the high school and junior high buildings immaculate. There were no leaky faucets, burned out light bulbs, everything worked perfectly all the time.

I loved practicing in the gym. It felt warm and safe, almost like a companion. The floors shined, perfectly clean. They projected, 'See how excellent I am. Can you be the same? Work and you can.' They spoke for Mr. Reynolds. He had pride in his work, every day demonstrating his goal of excellence.

Many will question custodial work making a difference. It did. There was no 'broken window syndrome' at our school, resulting in very few student disciplinary problems. Mr. Reynolds made the difference. He was respected by everyone as a role model in doing the best you possibly can, every day.

It is said, 10,000 hours of deliberate practice are required to become a master. It took me 10,000 hours to win the National Championship and be named Best in the World. However, it took far fewer hours to become world-class and named America's Favorite Cowgirl and Master of Visual and Verbal Communication. Once you learn how to rise to the top, repeat the process in all endeavors of your choice. It must be your choice, what you desire. It becomes a habit and touches all you do.

I give thanks to all my positive role models and especially those showing me excellence in their work. My ever-challenging goal of constant improvement serves me well. I call it 'divine discontent.' It leads to exciting discoveries and amazing satisfaction.

Are you hungry to discover all you can become using all you have been given? Grow and stretch, persist and discover. Do you pursue or pass? When you have reached your goal, do you hunker down or do you delight in reaching a new frontier and open doors to more? The hungry ones are those who take action and reach self-mastery, inspiring and leading others.

Those who fantasize living their lives as a caterpillar—eat a lot, sleep a while and wake up beautiful—are as emotionally immature as my praying at age 4 to wake up an Indian princess. Life gives back what we put in. The more that is returned to us, the more we can be of valued service to others.

> *"The quality of a person's life is in direct proportion to their commitment to excellence, regardless of their chosen field of endeavor."*
>
> -Vince Lombardi

CHOICES & FATE
Lead to your destiny.

Was it her tranquility and warm welcoming smile? Was it acknowledging the honor bestowed upon me? Or, a once-in-a-lifetime opportunity declined? I will never know the answer to why I remember in detail the picture of Dean LeBaron as I entered her office and our conversation.

I was asked to meet with her during my senior year at Iowa State. Iowa State and Cornell University were the top two Home Economics schools in the world. The lady who led her esteemed colleagues to excellence at Iowa State was Dean Helen LeBaron.

She asked me to be seated and proceeded to tell me why she requested our meeting. She wanted to improve the Home Economics curriculum. One improvement would be, instead of the required two years of core curriculum for all students before entering their field of interest, freshmen could immediately enter their field of interest while retaining the core curriculum.

She asked me to continue studies at Iowa State and help them with the new curriculum change. I would be head of changes for the psychological fields. I was shocked and quickly responded, "I'm not smart enough!"

"Yes, you are. You are smart enough and you are creative. We would like your help."

"But I am not wise enough." I truly thought I was not wise enough at 20 years old. How can I guide and teach others what I have not experienced, especially in family living and child development?

Dean LeBaron was a wise lady and knew I had other plans. She asked, "What are your plans? What are you planning to do?"

"I am going to twirl my batons."

She hesitated, smiled and said, "Joyce, I wish you all the best, we all do."

Dean LeBaron was often front-row with her professor friends during my performances at home basketball games. She had seen how I relentlessly created new routines and loved my work. She was the most accomplished and unassuming lady I have ever known.

Did I make the correct decision? There are pros and cons to every opportunity and decision. Hindsight is clearer. I told Dean LeBaron I was going to twirl my batons, but not why I couldn't accept her offer.

My junior year at Iowa State I was contracted to present school assemblies in the Midwest for two years following graduation. My assembly program was speaking on Physical Fitness and Mental Discipline and twirling my batons. The batons lent credibility and added entertainment.

The assembly work was physically taxing *and* the most rewarding I have ever experienced. Having young people come to you with faces glowing with hope, eyes seeing a vision of success, cannot be surpassed. That job gave me my life's direction—inspiring people to reach for their full potential! I had found my purpose and love.

Listen to your heart. Feel your instincts. When fate is directed by your heart and instincts, hallelujah!

I DARE YOU

I dare you to do something you have always wanted to do but lacked the courage. Not only will you have fun—you will feel a sense of freedom you will love. Robert Louis Stevenson said,

> *"To know what you prefer instead of humbly saying Amen to what the world tells you you ought to prefer, is to have kept your soul alive."*

Don't be a prisoner of society. As children are born and mature, they may become a prisoner of well-meaning parents, schools, marriages—doing jobs and activities they do not love or many times lack the needed abilities for. They soon become disenchanted, blaming themselves because they did what others wanted for them instead of what they wanted. Perhaps they didn't have the courage to do or even express what they wanted. If you are one of these people, my advice: Don't be bitter, make it better! Take action now!

The problem is not not *knowing* but rather not *doing* with what you know. Think of the skills you have and love to perform. How can they be adapted to an opportunity today?

If you are questioning your aptitude and love, think back to when you were a child, especially ages 7 to 17. What was your continuing dream, goal, magnificent obsession? Where did you develop talents because of your interest, drive and enthusiasm? What was easy because it was fun? What kept getting more fun the better you got? If your employment—or where you spend the major portion of your day—is one of those things or an offshoot, I'd be willing to bet you are happy. If you haven't found it, get busy and you will.

Success is doing what you love and loving what you do. But even love is seldom 100% pure. Getting to the big picture of love, there are a few things we must do that we don't love or even like. The secret to happiness is not always doing what we like, but learning to like what we have to do.

To get what we want from life, we must have the will to try, the faith to believe it is possible, and *work!*

YOUR FUTURE
It's your decision.

What is in your future? What do you envision? Instead of thinking, 'what if' think 'what's next?'

Be grateful for the talents, time, and life energy you have been granted.

Study success, don't copy it. Study the *Why*. Does the *What* fit you? *Who* are you? *What* do you want? Not all opportunities are right for you! Evaluate the pros and cons. Remember to always value yourself.

I received a phone call saying *The Tonight Show with Jay Leno* wanted me to appear in two weeks, doing the comedy routine I had done with Dom DeLuise on the *Mike Douglas Show*. They would replace Dom with Don Rickles. My first thought, Don Rickles! How could that work? His comedy style was very different from Dom's and mine.

I said, "Sorry. My daughter and I are contracted here in Salt Lake City and are not available for your date."

I was relieved. We had seen a male performer asked to do a 20-second spot on the *Tonight Show*, performing his signature trick. The man did a difficult and beautiful one finger stand. Jay asked his bandleader what he thought. The band leader did a thumbs down. Jay followed with his thumbs down. It was clear he didn't respect variety acts.

Two days later *The Tonight Show* booking agent called back determined I take the date. I again explained being contracted. He was noticeably frustrated. "You are turning down an opportunity to be seen by millions. What is needed to get you here?"

"Three things:

1. The amusement park in Salt Lake City may let us off for one day if they are publicly thanked. They must be thanked during my introduction.

2. My daughter and I are now working together. She must be on the show with me and a photo taken of Don, Jay, my daughter and myself for our publicity use.

3. I do a one-minute whip-cracking routine with my daughter singing Rawhide BEFORE the comedy bit."

I was confident that after the one-minute routine, Jay could not belittle my talent. It is important you respect yourself enough to protect yourself and not allow others to needlessly disrespect you. Respect builds and is lasting. Fame is fragile and fleeting. Never trade respect and dignity for fame.

I thought all was taken care of. They would never agree to my demands. To my surprise, the booking agent called the next day. "They accept all you want. We will email you the place, time and room reservations."

Long story short, it was stressful, but all worked out perfectly. They honored all my requests. Don Rickles was a great partner. He was funny, respectful, very complimentary and kind. *The Tonight Show* used a clip of Rickles and me with a whip as their teaser, netting them the most viewers of the show to date.

When the pros outweigh the cons and you approve, accept the opportunity! If the cons outweigh the pros, try to shift the balance. There is always a risk. Think positive common sense, not pie in the sky! Make it a win for all involved. If not, decline and move on.

Follow your heart and instincts. Do what you love and always with integrity. You create your future. Create rules, not wishes. Your future is dependent on your choices and actions. Be on the cutting edge. Risk being ahead of public acceptance. You can be the influencer, the leader, the change agent.

After assessing and determining what is required to reach your intended goal, adapt your capabilities, and Do it!

To reach your potential or to move the world, there are seven vital elements. They form an all-encompassing umbrella, blending together from the beginning to completion of Think it, Work it, Do it!

They are:

- Attitude—positive and 'can do'

- Purpose—*What?* and *Why?*

- Clarity—absolute

- Integrity—honest and excellent

- Focus—distraction free

- Persistence—unrelenting

- Gratitude—thankful and gracious

Keeping an accurate monthly evaluation system, rating each element on a scale from 0–10, is valuable for me and will be for you, your team and organization. Set an evaluation system to fit your improvement needs and goals. What needs improvement and how can it be done? What gets a gold star? There is nothing like seeing your progress or decline in black and white. Systematic evaluation keeps you consistent and your goals specific and in clear vision.

Go beyond what is expected, never settle for just adequate. Be exceptional. Losers say, "It may be possible but it is too difficult." Winners say, "It may be difficult, but it is possible." Be proactive and live your life to the fullest.

Happiness, health and longevity have a secret. The secret is not pursuing happiness! Henry James said,

"Three things are important.
The first thing is to be kind.
The second thing is to be kind.
The third thing is to be kind."

Studies show that those who practice kindness have better health, are happier, have better relationships, live longer and have more success in the workplace.

Wishing and striving for happiness leads to self-indulgent and self-absorbent. Kindness is forgotten. If you pursue kindness, empathy and doing for others is gained, and often creates happiness.

Teach children kindness. Teaching children happiness will lead to self-centeredness, entitlement and arrogance. As is true for all age groups. Many people focus on *getting* rather than *giving*. Which will you choose for you, your children and grandchildren? Giving kindness is a win-win for all involved.

Your mind creates thought. Your thoughts create your attitude and govern your beliefs. Your beliefs guide your actions. Your actions create your life.

Why not reverse the equation? Begin with behavior. Positive behaviors lead to positive attitudes. Positive attitudes lead to positive thoughts. Remember the James Lange theory? (William James, psychologist and Carl Lange, physiologist.)

> *"By acting and behaving in a cheerful manner, your thoughts and feelings will rush to keep up.'"*

The path to success is ever-changing and with it your vision for the future. What I have accomplished in my life is past, done and gone, but what I have learned will be with me a lifetime. Attributes for heightened success are focused dedication, preparation, and perseverance. And, fun! I will forever embrace challenges and continue to grow. I wish the same for you. May you be happy, focused and fearless!

May every 'hilltop' you reach speak to you,

> *"There is more, and you are free to go as far and high as you desire."*

With the solid earth beneath your feet, you are free to reach your magical unknown. You are capable, responsible and in control of your life!

Think it!

Work it!

Do it!

Acknowledgment

I am grateful to God and all those who taught, inspired, supported, and challenged me - all great leaders knowing *when* and *how* to lead.

About the Author

Joyce Rice is an inspiring and enthusiastic performer, author, and motivational speaker who connects to audiences of all ages through her genuine and generous spirit.

Featured nationally on ABC, CBS, and NBC, as well as numerous international television programs, Joyce has lectured on the "Art of Innovation" for such influential and forward-thinking corporations as General Dynamics, Rockwell International, and ITT.

Her self-developed strategies for success and happiness originated on her family's sixth-generation farm in Iowa and have been cultivated over a lifetime.

At age 17—after years of practice, determination and staying true to her potential—she was judged the best baton twirler in the world, defeating some 20,000 other young women for the World Champion title.

But that was just the beginning. She has also excelled in the field of entertainment with more than 40 years of experience on stage.

Her talent with the baton took her across the US and Europe, performing at professional football games, festivals, and world fairs and as the opening act for the Harlem Globetrotters.

She parlayed that talent into a long-running act as America's Favorite Cowgirl, demonstrating her prowess with whip-cracking, lariat-spinning, juggling, and comedy at venues around the world.

She also co-founded and developed the "Thank A Farmer" educational program, adding magic tricks to her repertoire to promote agriculture and the critical role of farmers and ranchers.

Joyce's numerous successes allow her to share with audiences how an Iowa farm girl with a dream became a successful innovator in show business—and one of today's most unique and outstanding speakers.

Her journey inspires her to engage with audiences and light a spark that will put people on the path of accomplishing their own dreams.

She's been called a "master of visual and verbal communication" and uses those skills to make points indelible and delight audiences by demonstrating innovation in action.

By sharing her life lessons and proven strategies, Joyce inspires and empowers others to maximize their talents, rise to the top, and live their full potential.

Joyce strives to help others remember they are capable, responsible, and in control of achieving their goals and dreams.

Made in the USA
Middletown, DE
13 July 2019